HU

IMAGES

Music in African-American Culture

VOLUME 1

Garland Reference Library of the Humanities

Volume 2089

Music in African-American Culture

Josephine Wright, *Series Editor*
Professor of Music and The Josephine Lincoln Morris Professor of Black Studies
The College of Wooster

IMAGES

Iconography of Music in African-American Culture, 1770s –1920s
by Eileen Southern and Josephine Wright

IMAGES

ICONOGRAPHY OF MUSIC IN AFRICAN-AMERICAN CULTURE, 1770s–1920s

Eileen Southern and
Josephine Wright

GARLAND PUBLISHING, INC.
New York and London

Published in 2000 by
Garland Publishing, Inc.
29 West 35th Street
New York, NY 10001

Published in London by
Garland Publishing, Inc.
11 New Fetter Lane
London EC4P 4EE

Garland is an imprint of the Taylor & Francis Group.

10 9 8 7 6 5 4 3 2 1

Library of Congress Cataloging-in-Publication Data

Southern, Eileen.
    Images : iconography of music in African-American culture (1770s–1920s) / by Eileen Southern and Josephine Wright.
        p. cm — (Music in African-American culture ; v. 1) (Garland reference library of the humanities ; vol. 2089)
    Includes bibliographical references (p.   ) and indexes.
    ISBN 0-8153-2875-3 (alk. paper)
        1. Afro-Americans—Music—Pictorial works.   2. Music in art.   I. Wright, Josephine 1942–.   II. Title.   III. Series.   IV. Series: Garland reference library of the humanities ; vol. 2089

    ML3556 .S738 2000
    780'.89'96073—dc21

                                                                00-029362

Printed on acid-free, 250-year-life paper
Manufactured in the United States of America

Contents

List of Illustrations

SERIES EDITOR'S FOREWORD

Music in African-American Culture

Josephine Wright

The music history of black America embraces a broad spectrum of musical styles, activities, and traditions, documented both in North America and abroad, at the earliest beginnings in the seventeenth century and continuing to the present day. These shared experiences help define African-Americans and their culture.

Volumes in this series will include monographs and edited collections of new essays that introduce recent research on all aspects of African-American music history, placing this rich and diverse heritage within a social, historical, and cultural context.

Acknowledgments

The iconography presented in this book was compiled under a grant from the National Endowment for the Humanities, with supportive funding from The College of Wooster's Henry Luce Award for Distinguished Scholarship for payment of all permission fees.

A number of persons contributed significantly to this project over the past decade, and to all we are deeply indebted: professional photographers Kurt Muller, Lydia Dull, Rick Stafford, and Michael Nedweski took special care in making copies of our collection's old prints and engravings; and Mary Katherine Donaldson, American art historian, served as secretary and computer researcher, and her secure knowledge provided a reliable guide through the sometimes treacherous water of music iconography. From time to time Harvard graduate students, particularly Lewis Porter and Christopher Johnson, joined the research team. From our colleagues in history, art history, and music history we received advice and encouragement—especially from the late Lorenzo Johnston Greene and Howard Mayer Brown, as well as from Sterling Stuckey, David Driskell, Sarah Burns, and John Ward. Many librarians, archivists, and audiovisual technicians helped us locate obscure sources and obtain photographic reproductions of artworks. In that regard, we wish to thank the personnel of the Boston Museum of Fine Arts, the Boston Public Library, the Cleveland Public Library, Harvard University Libraries, the Library of Congress, Oberlin College Libraries, the Moorland-Spingarn Research Center, the New York Public Library, and The College of Wooster.

Introduction

It is only within the last two decades that scholars studying African-American slavery and its culture have begun to appreciate the importance of the primary documentation offered by the slaves' traditional oral literature, music, and dance and by their written personal records, particularly the autobiographies. Now it is generally accepted that despite the oppressive rigors and brutality of slavery, the plantation infrastructure made possible, for most slaves at least, some small measure of freedom, at one time or another, from the surveillance of the slaveholder. During this time they were free to create their own social universe, in which they had control of important events in their lives, if only temporarily.

To gain access to that world, historians have relied on the usual sources available in the white community: plantation records; diaries, journals, and other personal documents; newspaper and magazine materials; imaginative literature; travelogues and more; and additionally of course the slave materials mentioned above. However, an important source of information apparently has been overlooked by researchers, and that is visual representation of the African-American's cultural activities. Scholars reconstructing the historical past of slave culture seem not yet to recognize the value of using visual materials not just as illustrations for their texts or support for their theses, but also for the evidence contained in their subject matter.[1]

In this book we propose to approach the subject matter from the perspective of a historian of the traditional performing arts (music, dance, and religious and secular oral literature), permitting the visual image to tell its own story and arriving at conclusions based on the information it provides, holding in special regard information confirmed by contemporaneous literary sources and/or oral tradition. In short, this is not a social history in pictures of black-American culture or a pictorial record of African-American achievement in the nineteenth century. Rather, it focuses on identifying, describing, and analyzing the cultural art forms and activities represented in the pictorial records that lie at the roots of African-American traditional culture. It is an iconography of black culture that includes photographic reproduction of the artworks on which it is based.

The idea for this project came to my colleague, Josephine Wright, and me more than a decade ago, while we were preparing for publication our work *African-American Traditions in Song, Sermon, Tale, and Dance, 1600s–1920: An Annotated Bibliography of Literature, Collections, and Artworks* (published in 1990). Impressed by the number of illustrations we came across in contemporary magazines and books that depicted aspects of black culture, we decided to compile a collection of artworks to serve as a companion to the bibliography. But there had to be an ordering of the visual materials, an identification of a theme or themes, and the establishment of a basis for categorizing the pictures. Finally, we resolved to let the material itself determine its course: we would systematically collect genre pictures depicting African-American traditional culture in the nineteenth century, with the expectation that themes would emerge as our gatherings increased in number.

Although this was a collaborative project from the outset, it soon became obvious that if ever we were to complete the research for a study of such large dimensions, at some point we would have to divide the labors; consequently, Professor Wright took major reponsibility for the archival research, while I assumed responsibility for sorting out the research findings and writing the text. Through the years we have continuously exchanged ideas about procedures and content, revised the text again and again, and searched exhaustively for solutions to troubling problems. The completed work is truly a fusion of both our ideas and our aspirations.

Of the hundreds of artworks we examined, we chose 260, representing various media and kinds of subject matter, for inclusion in this book. Early on it became obvious that although nineteenth-century artists found some themes more appealing than others, the commissions they received, their conditions of employment, and the marketplace all played a part in determining the subject matter that the artists chose to depict. Nevertheless, the samplings of the artworks depicting any single theme associated with African-American culture were large enough to allow for an ordering of the pictures in historical-social-cultural context according to, first, chronological position and, second, thematic content.

The book is divided into three parts: Part I consists of a gathering of artworks that represent black Americans in the colonial and federalist eras, Part II covers artworks depicting traditional black culture in the antebellum era, and Part III covers artworks from the time of the Civil War to the end of World War I. Of course, for African-Americans the great divide was crossed not with the Civil War but with the Emancipation Proclamation (1863) and the passage of the Thirteenth Amendment (1865), which finally freed all the nation's slaves.

Although the artworks themselves are reproduced in the book in numerical order according to visual themes and interesting juxtapositions, discussion of many works appears in several places throughout the book, so figures are not necessarily referred to in the text in numerical order. The List of Illustrations in the front of the book and the Index of Artwork by Title and Index of Artists in the back of the book will help the reader easily locate each figure.

In preparation for the first phase of the project—collecting the pictures—we established three criteria. First, we decided the pictures should be genre works; that is, they should depict black Americans in scenes of their everyday life. The term "everyday life," however, need not be limiting, but could apply to scenes that involved blacks in public events, such as political gatherings or parades, or in a re-creation of a historical event. The term also could apply to fiction, or "literary genre" produced by an artist who drew his or her figures from imaginative writings, such as Joel Chandler Harris's Uncle Remus and Br'er Rabbit tales.

Second, the images should show blacks in their own private social world, from which whites were excluded or relegated to marginal positions, as, for example, when they are depicted as spectators in the background at social events of the blacks. To be sure, in a few instances where scenes refer to some important aspect of white activity, they have been included because of their historical or social-cultural value.

Finally, the images should focus on the centrality of traditional music for the black community, as performed by self-taught folk musicians. Almost immediately it became apparent that this third rule would have to be altered, not because of the scarcity of images of music-making, but because few pictures show music as the central activity. Most often music is integrated with other activities, such as the dance, or is performed concurrently with another activity, such as in the worship service. Consequently, rather than limit the search to music-making, we decided to widen it to include any scene depicting black-American expressive culture. For convenience we include the dance among the expressive culture forms, for although obviously not oral literature, it has its own characteristic language and distinctive mode of communication, and its function as an African-American performing art is similar in many ways to that of the song.

The special nature of African-American traditional culture, because of its fusion of African and European elements, required an unorthodox approach to examination of its iconography. The method that we have improvised to meet the needs of this study is indebted to several disciplines, most importantly musicology, ethnomusicology, musical iconography, and art history, particularly the writings of Erwin Panofsky.[2]

Examination of the art materials has involved three stages. On the primary level, our aim was to describe the pictures, identifying their content and natural subject matter. The second level called for analysis, a searching for the intrinsic meaning of the activity represented in the picture and for thematic relationships among the artworks, which would permit classification of the works and the grouping of those works that embody the same themes. It was at this level that resort to literature of the period and/or oral tradition proved to be useful in our efforts to corroborate data left vague or incomprehensible in the picture.

The third level, requiring interpretation of the subject matter in terms of its historical-cultural-social significance and explanation of its impact on national and world culture, we determined lay outside the scope of the present investigation, although in a few instances we touched on such matters for compelling reasons. It is our opinion that such study belongs more properly within the purview of the social-science disciplines.

Of the several questions for which we sought answers, the following seemed most important: (1) the role of expressive culture and dance in the black community; (2) the special role of culture in the black church; (3) the performance practice (i.e., conventions) of singing, dancing, instrumental music, preaching, and storytelling; (4) the kinds of musical instruments used; and (5) the relationships between selected African-American cultural elements and their African prototypes.

In representing black bondsmen (and later, the freedmen), nineteenth-century artists drew on the established traditions of American genre painting. The same stock figures that artists presented in scenes of everyday life of white Americans—farm workers, itinerant peddlers, card players, roustabouts, domestic workers, and so on—reappeared in works of art featuring black figures, except the latter were placed in settings associated with the black community, such as plantations, rural villages, city street corners, and docks and wharves. Similarly, artists used the same themes in their pictorial recording of the special events attended by blacks and whites—country dances, corn-husking frolics and other kinds of rural festivities, hunting, election and political gatherings, children at play, country weddings, parades, etc. Some themes, however, may have been unique to the black community—for example, "the black preacher" and "the Negro burial," which apparently had no counterparts in the genre paintings of white folk.

In conceptualizing and realizing these themes, artists used a variety of formats. About one-fifth of our collected pictures consists of oil paintings, ranging in size from Eastman Johnson's small "Negro Boy" (c. 1860, 14 × 17⅛ inches) to Samuel Jennings's immense "Liberty Displaying the Arts and Sciences" (1792, 60¼ × 73⅛ inches). The large majority of the works in our collection are engravings, which, like the paintings, originally were various sizes—some small enough to fit into the width of a magazine column, others so large as to fill the pages of contemporary magazines (9 × 14 inches) or double pages (14 × 20 inches). The illustrated press of the nineteenth century was fond of publishing "pictorial essays" (independently of text) in the form of strip sequences of several prints that traced the development of a story. (For the purposes of this study, pictures were enlarged or reduced as necessary in order to give the utmost clarity to the subject matter.)

It would have been futile to attempt to trace the origins of the various artworks. Some works that first were executed as paintings later were reproduced as engravings and distributed to the public through mail orders from printed catalogs. Some works originally commissioned by writers as book illustrations were passed from one book to the next, with alterations freely entered along the way. Sometimes illustrators had not personally seen the images they developed into engravings, having made their sketches on the basis of detailed eyewitness reports. This was especially common among "combat artists" during the Civil War, as also was the practice of using photographs as "models" for paintings and engravings.

To arrive at a precise count of the number of artists whose works are reproduced here is impossible (see Index of Artists). While 115 names can be definitely associated with artworks (some artists are represented by many works), thirty-three pictures are anonymous, and several pictures have been signed by two or more names. In any event, the artists include the most eminent American painters of the nineteenth and early twentieth centuries, among them Thomas Eakins, Charles Demuth, Eastman Johnson, Winslow Homer, and William Sidney Mount, as well as men who were well known and successful in their time but are forgotten now. About two dozen artists were born abroad and later immigrated to the United States, twelve from Great Britain alone. Artists immigrated also from Germany, France, and other countries on the continent. As for the Americans, most were born in the Northeast, but no fewer than five were natives of the South. To be sure, since biographical details are missing for large numbers of the artists, as well as the anonymous ones, it is possible that the actual geographical distribution of the artists differed from our approximation. Finally, it should be noted that no fewer than four women artists are represented in our collection, and there is reason to believe that some of the anonymous works are attributable to women.

As a group the artists were well trained according to the standards of the day: some attended the National Academy of Design in New York, the Pennsylvania Academy of Fine Arts, or smaller academies, or studied privately; some studied abroad in Paris at the École des Beaux-Arts, the Dusseldorf Academy, and privately. Few of them were able to earn a secure livelihood as independent artists, but they found employment with the illustrated press, particularly *Frank Leslie's Illustrated Newspaper, Harper's New Monthly*

Magazine, Harper's Weekly, New York Illustrated Magazine, and *Scribner's Monthly Magazine* (later renamed *Century Magazine*) as staff artists or "special artists." Several chose teaching careers, serving as art professors in liberal arts colleges or teachers in art academies. And they secured commissions to portray African-Americans from authors of the fiction and nonfiction that flooded the nation, particularly after the Civil War. The fortunate ones also obtained patronage from art academies, of which the National Academy of Design in New York City (founded in 1826) was most influential, with its annual exhibitions of paintings produced by its members, and from art unions, particularly the Apollo Association in New York City (established 1838, later reorganized as the American Art-Union). In summary, it would appear that our artists, as specialists in genre painting and engraving, were admirably fitted for constructing scenes that depicted the details of everyday life for African-Americans, and that their works should have met no difficulties in finding purchasers.

That indeed was true. But questions arise concerning the qualifications of the artists for capturing the essential character of a people about whom they knew so little. All were white Americans or Europeans, most of whom had had scant contact, if any at all, with black folk before beginning their professional careers—with one exception, the African-American genre painter Henry Ossawa Tanner. Normally, it is assumed that the culture of a people reflects its values and beliefs, that the cultural forms of a people represent its creative expression based on its own experience, not that of outsiders. It is an anomaly, therefore, that we must witness the emergence and development of African-American culture through the eyes of the white artist insofar as the pictorial record is concerned. To be sure, this dilemma is not unique to the graphic arts: the slave songs were first gathered and published by white musicians, and the Br'er Rabbit tales were first collected and published by whites. Nineteenth-century collectors of slave lore were sensitive to the possible charges that they might be unqualified to carry out the work they had assigned themselves: the song- and tale-gatherers asserted they had transcribed the oral literature exactly as they heard it from the lips of the slaves; the artists, that they had painted or drawn from models precisely as they saw them; and the writers, that their books were "records of facts," not "works of fiction."

Though African-Americans generally represented unknown quantities to white artists in the early antebellum era, the situation began to change in the 1850s with the growth of the nation's illustrated press and the emergence of a new order of artists, the "artist-reporter" and the "pictorial-journalist." The public seems to have had an intense curiosity about the black men and women in their midst, whose existence threatened the destruction of the nation, and publishers sent their reporters near and far in search of stories, accompanied by artists who made sketches on the spot. Further, the artists' press assignments and book commissions took them "behind the race curtain" into person-to-person contacts with the African-Americans who would be serving as models for paintings, prints, and drawings—on the plantations, on dusty country roads, in the rural churches, at the camp meetings, on the docksides and wharves, and in the battlefields as both contraband and servicemen once the war had begun. Additionally, some artists undoubtedly were inspired to paint images of black folk by their personal curiosity or the pull of the exotic.

Finally, then, our purpose in this book is to appraise the character of African-American traditional culture in the nineteenth century as it is represented in selected genre paintings, prints, drawings, and photographs. Evaluating a work of art in terms of its subject matter and the evidence it provides sometimes reveals information that is unobtainable in any other way, thus supplementing knowledge obtained from literary and archival sources. Moreover, if there are enough images that show African-Americans working, singing, dancing, performing on musical instruments, celebrating rites of passage, and worshiping God in time-honored rituals, these images inevitably will reflect the values and beliefs of the people and offer penetrating insight into the role of expressive culture in their daily lives, no matter who the artist.

Eileen Southern

Notes

1. For convenience of discussion, we use the term "artwork" or "work of art" to identify any form of graphic creative expression, with no concern for the quality of the product. Both professionals and amateurs are represented here; their oil paintings, engravings, watercolors, drawings, photographs, and other graphic art forms appear side by side, without regard for the eminence of the artists who produced them. Regarding the subject matter or purpose of the artworks, the serious, political, historical, and personal composition, and even the caricature are included if their subject matter is relevant to the purpose of our study. Works cited in abbreviated form in the notes are given in full in the bibliography.

2. See Panofsky, 26–42. Among the other studies that influenced our developing a methodology for studying these artworks are Howard M. Brown, *Musical Iconography;* Patricia Hills, *The Painter's America;* Elizabeth Johns, *American Genre Painting;* Richard Leppert, *Music and Image. . . . ;* and articles published in *Imago Musicae.*

IMAGES

PART I

THE COLONIAL AND FEDERALIST ERAS

The African Legacy

The Africans who, beginning in 1619, were sold into slavery and shipped to the mainland of colonial North America were stripped to the skin and shackled in chains for the long, traumatic voyage across the Atlantic Ocean, the so-called Middle Passage. Though prohibited from carrying material possessions with them, they retained memories of the rich cultural traditions of the motherland, and, after being settled in their new home, they gave evidence of this in many ways, particularly in how they observed their religious ceremonies and spent their leisure time. Enslavement effected the breakup of families—separating husbands and wives from each other and parents from children—as well as the dissolution of tribal and national ties, which created language barriers, but the transplanted Africans nevertheless found ways to communicate with each other through their traditional expressive arts. Nowhere was this more obvious than at the mammoth slave festivals that occurred periodically during the slave-trade period (c. 1650s–1850s) in places where large numbers of Africans were concentrated on the mainland of English-speaking North America.[1]

Slave Festivals in the Colonies

White colonists watched the dancing of the Africans and listened to their singing with a mixture of admiration, disparagement, and outright disapproval. Nevertheless, some of the whites included accounts of the African-style festivities in their travelogues, journals, local histories, diaries and other personal writings, and fiction. In New England it was the 'Lection Day festival, which took place in late May or June, that drew hundreds of slaves to a temporary "capital," where they elected a "king" or "governor" for the coming year, paraded in full display accompanied by bands, and spent the remainder of the time in merrymaking. In New York State, particularly at Albany and New York City, but also in other Dutch communities, it was the Pinkster festival, which began the Monday after Pentecost Sunday and continued for several days, that attracted huge crowds of white and black spectators to watch slaves playing African musical instruments and dancing as they (or their ancestors) had danced in Africa. In Philadelphia the slaves carried on their "jubilees" during the time the city held its semiannual fairs—dancing in the city's Potter's Field (the public burial ground, now Washington Square), the blacks joyful above while the dead reposed below. "In that field could be seen at once more than one thousand of both sexes, divided into numerous little squads, dancing and singing in their own tongue, after the customs of their several nations in Africa."[2] Finally, there was the exotic slave dancing that took place on Sunday afternoons in the Place Congo of New Orleans, Louisiana, which was obligatory sight-seeing for tourists and, as well, for natives of the city. We shall return later to discussion of these festivals.

European Explorers and Traders

At the same time as white American colonists were beginning to take note of the African festivals in their midst, European explorers and traders in West Africa were keeping records of their adventures among the Yoruba, Hausa, Ashanti, Ibo, Fon, and other, primarily West African, nations, with a view to publishing their notes or diaries in book format after returning to their homes. Beginning as early as 1620 and continuing through the eighteenth and mid-nineteenth centuries, these writers include comment on the music and dance of West Africa, some in greater detail than others. Examining the data as presented by one writer after another gives considerable insight into such matters as the role of music in African society, performance practice, instrumentation, private and public ceremonies, and the interrelationship between music and dance and other cultural traditions—this, despite the unavoidable "outsider" viewpoints of the European writers, and the paucity of books published by the Africans themselves.

Evidence of Pictorial Records

Several of the publications of the explorers and traders proved to be invaluable for the present study, because they include engravings and drawings that show genre scenes of Africans making music, dancing, and participating in various kinds of ceremonies. Even more important, the artworks complement the verbal descriptions of these activities that are found in literature of the period. The small collection of artworks gathered from those publications and presented here offers pictorial evidence of the kinds of traditions practiced by the Africans during the slave-trade era, and it reveals a number of basic similarities between African and African-American cultural traditions during the same period. Although the African pictures generally tell their own stories, we nevertheless will quote liberally from relevant contemporaneous literature in the interest of placing events in the appropriate context. In later discussion of African-American traditions, we shall have occasion to refer back to the African prototypes and traditions represented in these pictures.

Importance of Music and Dance

Above all, the European writers were impressed by the important role played by music and dance in African society. One of the earliest observations on the subject comes from English sea captain Richard Jobson, who writes in 1620, after exploring the Gambia River region, "There is without doubt, no people on earth more naturally affected to the sound of musicke than these people; which the principall persons do hold as an ornament of their state, so as when wee come to see them their musicke will seldome be wanting."[3]

This comment or a similar one appears again and again in contemporary literature. In 1789, Olaudah Equiano, an African, expresses essentially the same belief from the African viewpoint: "We are almost a nation of dancers, musicians, and poets. . . . Thus every great event, such as a triumphant return from battle or other cause of public rejoicing, is celebrated in public dances, which are accompanied with songs and music suited to the occasion."[4]

There is no question of the primacy of the dance in the lifestyle of the West Africans. Through the dance they could communicate with each other and with their deities, and the European spectators felt its power. John Atkins notes:

> Dancing is the Diversion of their Evenings: Men and Women make a ring in an open part of the town, and one at a time shews his skill in Antick Motions and Gesticulations, yet with a great deal of Agility, the Company making the Musicke by clapping their hands together.

Captain Hugh Clapperton notes:

> Towards evening, each day, the sound of the drum calls them to the open space in the center of their huts, when the men form themselves into circles and dance in a most uncouth though joyous manner.

Alexander Laing notes:

> Dancing is a favorite amusement among [them] . . . the musicians (if
> they may be so called) stand in the centre, while the men and women,
> mixed indiscriminately together, dance around them, but with little
> change of place, as the movements are principally confined to the head
> and upper parts of the body.

Francis Moore points out:

> [They] will dance to a Drum or a Balafeu sometimes four and twenty
> Hours together, dancing now and then very regular, and at other Times
> in very odd gestures, striving always to outdo one another in Nimbleness
> and Activity.[5]

The various discussions in the Europeans' journals of music and dance performance practice inevitably include detailed description of the musical
instruments, in regard not only to how the music is performed but also to how
the instruments are constructed, how they are combined with other instruments, and how they function in the context of the music and dance situation.
The writers give English names to the instruments they most often encountered—the drums of various sizes, flutes and fifes, fiddles, banjos, horns, trumpets, and the balafou, among others—or use African names in anglicized
forms.

Three pictures in our little collection of African scenes focus on individual
musical instruments, of which two depict "singing men" or jellemen playing
their instruments (figs. 2 and 3), and one is a chart drawing of instruments
commonly found among West African nations (fig. 4).[6] Directions for constructing these instruments appear in most of the books we examined, though
the names given to them vary from source to source.

A fourth instrumental-music scene (fig. 1) represents the kind of band that
typically attended a chief or king when he left his castle to "go abroad"; or, perhaps it represents the first line of march in a procession. No special terms are
used in the literature to apply to the long trumpets depicted here (which are
made of wood or other natural materials). Evidently the instruments were so
well known at the time as not to require special comment. (See pp. 190–91, 250,
252 regarding "long trumpets" in the antebellum and postbellum periods of
the United States.)

Ceremonies and Rituals

Both "Funeral Ceremony at Annabon" (fig. 6) and "Bota-Kim-Mo" (fig. 7)
are genre prints, with stories that have religious references. William Allen and

FIGURE 1. [Trumpets and Drums.] Early-20th-c. Photograph. Schomburg Center for Research in Black Culture, Photographs and Prints Division, New York Public Library, Astor, Lenox and Tilden Foundations.

FIGURE 2. "Jelleman of Soolimana [and] Jelleman of Kooranko." Hand-colored print. Published in *Travels in the Timannee, Kooranko, and Soolima Countries in Western Africa*, by Alexander Gordon Laing. London: John Murray, 1825.

FIGURE 3. "Jellemen of Soolimana." Hand-colored print. Published in *Travels in the Timannee, Kooranko, and Soolima Countries in Western Africa*, by Alexander Gordon Laing. London: John Murray, 1825.

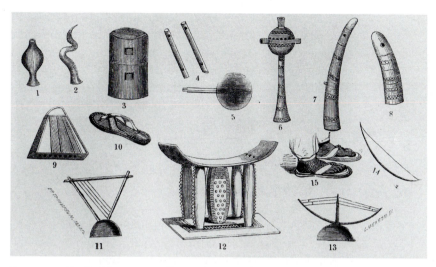

FIGURE 4. D. B. Thompson. "Description of the Instruments." Engraving by G. Measom. Published in *A Narrative of the Expedition Sent by Her Majesty's Government to the River Niger in 1841 . . .* , by William Allen and T. R. H. Thomson. London: Richard Bentley, 1848.

T. R. H. Thomson, authors of the book in which the funeral scene is found, are somewhat cynical about the rite under performance but admit it to be "picturesque." They explain their presence at the ceremony: "We witnessed part of a funeral ceremony for a woman who had died the evening before. . . . All the people were found assembled in a semi-circle at the front of a house, singing, or rather screeching, most hideously. A man in the middle poised a cross at least twenty-feet high, which was rather a difficult performance for, being as thin as a lath, it required the greatest dexterity to keep it from bending."[7]

Continuing their account, Allen and Thomson note that the male holding the cross is surrounded by a circle of ugly old women, attired in white, who wave branches to and fro "as they shuffle about, to the sound of drums and their own discordant voices."

The artist, J. W. Cook, taking a more sensitive approach to the ritual, depicts a sympathetic image of a typical village funeral, which calls to viewer attention some features distinctively African, such as the ring dance, the drumming, and the mourners loudly expressing their grief in song. The presence of the two crosses, the one held by the male dancer in the center of the circle and the other, an enormous one planted outside the circle, suggest this to be an Africanized Christian rite or, to quote Allen and Thomson, "a mixture of Fetichism and Christianity."[8]

The other ceremonial picture (fig. 7) shows a "chanting priest," Bota-Kim-Mo, preparing to take his men, about two hundred in number, on a big hunt. Fastening a large net to trees nearby to form an enclosure, they have readied the trap into which they will drive the animals. In this scene Bota-Kim-Mo is begging the deity Rupi to come to his aid: he has lit a fire and is dancing with uplifted spear as he calls out loudly to Rupi, "his numerous companions joining their voices in rude chorus." As he danced, "his features become contorted, his body covered with perspiration from his exertions, and he looked like a person out of his senses."[9] Clearly, the priest is possessed by the spirits. But we know from the text that his prayers soon will be answered, the hunt will get underway, and the outcome will be successful.

The Annual "Customs"

Most tribes commemorated an annual festival, called a "Custom," in association with the harvesting of the tribe's national fruit or vegetable. A mixture of public ceremony, carnival, religious ritual, military exercise, and other kinds of public events, the celebrations drew participants from miles around and could last for several days or up to several weeks. Generally, this event was called simply the Annual Custom, but among the Ashanti (and others) it was called the Yam Custom in honor of their beloved vegetable, the yam (a member of the sweet-potato family).[10] Thanks to Englishman Thomas Edward Bowdich, a record of the celebration in 1818 is preserved in a watercolor painting (fig. 8) he made while in Ashanti on a commercial mission for the African Committee of London and later published in his book *Mission from Cape Coast Castle to Ashantee* (1819).

Bowdich uses a full chapter to describe the procession on the opening day of the festival and, even so, occasionally seems at a loss for words to describe the magnificence of the scene. His painting is filled to overflowing with musicians, warriors, dancers, chiefs and their retinues, English visitors and other spectators, and the king. Every conceivable kind of musical instrument is represented, including the exotic long flutes and long trumpets. Bowdich's text, closely aligned with the picture, relates in great detail the happenings of the first day of the Custom and his personal reaction to the events.

The Centrality of African Song

Although it appears that the European writers gave their primary attention to the dance and instrumental music, undoubtedly because of the novelty of the instrumental performances, they were not oblivious to the omnipresence of vocal music and its traditions among the people. Many instances are cited where communication is carried on entirely through song: the praise singers, for example, improvise songs in honor of their patrons, the singing men recite the historical events of the nation (figs. 2 and 3). Predictably, singing plays an indispensable role in worship events; indeed, as William Hutchison wrote in his diary in 1818, "[The Africans] conceive to worship God in any other way than chaunting [*sic*] or singing is absurd."[11]

Vocal music of course has its characteristic forms of expression, of which the most frequently encountered is the call-and-response pattern. Captain Clapperton, one of many writers who comments on the musical form, was struck by the contrast between "call" and "response" in a performance he heard where two bards (accompanied by two drummers) sang the praises of their master, "one responding in a clear, shrill voice the words of the chorus, while the other sang, or rather bawled aloud [the lyrics of the verses]."[12]

The explorers observed also another characteristic feature of African song: some types of vocal performance integrated speech and song; some types integrated speech and what might be loosely defined as "musical noises." Examples of the latter are especially associated with gatherings where the format is that of a group listening to a speaker, as at the village palaver meeting represented here (fig. 5). Every small village had periodic meetings of its council, or

FIGURE 5. J. W. Cook. "A Palaver." Engraving. Published in *A Narrative of the Expedition Sent by Her Majesty's Government to the River Niger in 1841 . . .* , by William Allen and T. R. H. Thomson. London: Richard Bentley, 1848.

FIGURE 6. J. W. Cook. "Funeral Ceremony at Annabon." Engraving. Published in *A Narrative of the Expedition Sent by Her Majesty's Government to the River Niger in 1841 . . .* , by William Allen and T. R. H. Thomson. London: Richard Bentley, 1848.

FIGURE 7. D. B. Thompson. "Bota-Kim-Mo, or Chanting Priest Invoking the Moh's Before a Hunt." Engraving. Published in *A Narrative of the Expedition Sent by Her Majesty's Government to the River Niger in 1841 . . .* , by William Allen and T. R. H. Thomson. London: Richard Bentley, 1848.

palaver, where minor problems were discussed and solved, and every so often a grand palaver was held, to which the village palavers sent delegates. Theophilus Conneau observes that at the palavras [*sic*] "it is the custom [for those who listen] to give a groan or sigh at any remarkable or affecting description, and [to] use the same gutteral groan in token of assent," for no one is allowed to interrupt the speaker.[13]

J. W. Cook's engraving, "A Palaver" (fig. 5), offers a picture of the village council that is almost photographic in its realistic detail. The viewer can feel the intensity of the discussion, which involves women as well as men, and it is certain that the "groans and sighs" will be forthcoming with great ardor.

Notes

1. In 1807, Congress passed a law prohibiting the importation of African slaves into the United States after January 1, 1808, but illegal trafficking in slavery flourished into the 1860s. Moreover, there was vigorous trading within the United States among the Southern states throughout the antebellum period. One of the best known of the slave traders, Theophilus Conneau, did not even begin his twenty-year activity until 1819, nine years after slavery was abolished by law.
2. Watson, *Annals,* 265.
3. Jobson, *Golden Trade,* 105.
4. Equiano, *Interesting Narrative,* 3.
5. Atkins, *Voyage,* 53; Clapperton, *Narrative* 2:58; Laing, *Travels,* 104; Moore, *Travels,* 110.
6. Various names are used by the explorers to refer to the professional musicians or "singing men" they wrote about in their travel journals, such as jelleman, jillikea, griot, bard, minstrel, and troubadour.
7. Allen, *Narrative,* 2:53–54.
8. Ibid., 2:53.
9. Ibid., 2:213.
10. Ibid., 2:397. Allen notes that the Yam Custom is one which "nearly all the tribes adhere to . . . and the manner in which it is carried out . . . evinces that it must have had its origin from one and the same source."
11. Hutchison in Bowdich, *Mission,* 414.
12. Clapperton, *Narrative,* 2:233.
13. Conneau, *Slaver's Log Book,* 136.

FIGURE 8. Thomas Edward Bowdich. "The First Day of the Yam Custom." Hand-colored print. Engraving by R. Havell & Son. Published in *Mission from Cape Coast Castle to Ashantee, with a Statistical Account of That Kingdom . . . ,* by T. Edward Bowdich. London: John Murray, 1819.

FIGURE 8. Thomas Edward Bowdich. "The First Day of the Yam Custom" (*continued*)

Everyday Slave Life
in the United States

Little is known about "The Old Plantation" (fig. 9), the earliest genre painting in United States history to depict African-American culture, except
that this watercolor was discovered in Columbia, South Carolina, and is
believed to have originated on a plantation situated between Charleston and
Orangeburg, South Carolina.[1] Judging by the English watermarks, it could be
assumed that the paper was manufactured at some time during the years 1777
to 1794, thus allowing a late-eighteenth-century date for the watercolor.

The scene shows a large plantation: in the foreground twelve adults, six men
and six women, are dancing, apparently singing, and otherwise making merry
in a clearing in front of two slave cabins; in the middle ground (representing a
great distance from the foreground) slave oarsmen are rowing boats on a wide
river; and in the background are the other plantation buildings—the Big
House (residence of the slaveholding family), service houses, and a row of
slave cabins.

Obviously, the gathering is a festive occasion for the slaves, who are dressed
in their finest, except for the absence of shoes (field hands do not wear shoes),
and a pervasive cheerfulness infuses the entire scene. Significantly, the affair
takes place far from the prying eyes of the slavemaster and his overseer, thus
allowing the slaves the freedom to celebrate their holiday in any way they
choose.

Five of the celebrators are totally involved with the dancing: two women
dancers wave scarves, holding the ends between their index fingers and thumbs;
a male dancer grasps a stick with both hands as he jumps from one foot to the
other; and the two musicians produce music on a long-neck, four-string

17

FIGURE 9. "The Old Plantation." Late 18th–c. watercolor. 11¾ × 18 in. Abby Aldrich
Rockefeller Folk Art Center, Williamsburg, Virginia (acc. no. 35.301.3).

gourd-banjo and a small drum wedged between the drummer's legs, which he
beats with two tiny sticks. Some of the merrymakers have wide-open mouths,
as if singing loudly—or it may be that they have just taken quaffs of wine (or
something stronger) from the jug planted at the banjoist's feet and are laughing off its influence. This image of a slave banjo well may be the earliest illustration in history of the African-American instrument, with its three full
strings and a fourth "short string" set into the neck at a halfway point between
the bridge and the nut.[2] It is noteworthy that descriptions of instruments similar to this one are found in journals and travelogues published by European
explorers both in Africa and in the Caribbean during the slave-trade period.

Though the slave revelers wear American colonial-style dress, their dancing
and musical performance point to an African origin; indeed, it is possible that
the slaves themselves were born in Africa, and that their performance represents
a continuation of the practices of their homeland in the new South Carolina
home. The descriptions of African music and dance in contemporaneous
travel books offer striking agreement with the pictorial evidence of "The Old
Plantation." In Mederic Moreau de Saint-Mery's *Dance* (1797), for example,
the author observes that in the Kalenda [*sic*], a couple dance of African origin,

"the lady holds the corners of a handkerchief which [she] waves," and in the Chica, the lady "holds the corners of a handkerchief or the two ends of her apron."[3] Further, a traveler in Central Africa notes that the women "place a blue wrapper or scarf over the shoulders, and hold each end of the wrapper with arms extended" as they dance.[4]

Also in colonial-period travel literature are references to the energetic male stick dance as one "performed by men armed with sticks, who springing alternately from one foot to another, while dancing round in a ring, frequently flourished their sticks in the air or clashed them together with a loud noise."[5] As for the musical forces represented in this watercolor, it was common to find the gourd-banjo and small drum combined to form an ensemble for African dancing. In 1623, explorer Richard Jobson observed that in Gambia, "That [instrument] which is most common in use, is made of a great gourd, and a necke thereunto fastened, resembling in some sort, our Bandora. . . . In consortship with this they have many times another who playes upon a little drumme . . . which he holds under his left arme, and with a crooked stick in his right hand, and his naked fingers on the left he strikes the drumme."[6]

In some places small boys were called upon to contribute to the musical ensemble of banjo and small drum, as in Guinea, where "they set a little Boy to strike upon a hollow piece of Iron with a piece of Wood," and in Dahomey, where "the boys had hollow gourds with stones or beans in them, with which they kept time by holding them in one hand and beating them against the other."[7] And the custom was prevalent as well in the United States: English traveler John F. D. Smyth, watching a "negroe dancer" in Virginia in 1784, marveled at how he was "keeping time and cadence, most exactly, with the music of a large banjor (a large hollow instrument with three strings) and a quaqua (somewhat resembling a drum)."[8]

It is obvious that the unknown painter of "The Old Plantation" has made considerable efforts to individualize the faces of the revelers, and a perceptive viewer might even discern family resemblances among the slaves. This is a picture that must be read on more than one level: first, it is a genre painting, fixing a moment in the everyday life of twelve slaves on a plantation in South Carolina; second, it is a depiction of a music and dance performance on a Southern plantation; third, it is a representation of the merging of African and European elements in the African-American dance; and, finally, it is a pictorial record of twelve individuals drawn together in a group portrait, perhaps a "family" group.[9]

That the folk artist was more concerned about producing good likenesses of his subjects than obeying laws of anatomical drawing is indicated in the way he handled the figures in the second row: none are given bodies below the waist level to support their strikingly detailed torsos. There is a real possibility that the artist might have been a slave musician in view of his scrupulous attention to details that undoubtedly would have been passed over by one who was not an insider—the way, for example, the female dancers hold their scarves and the male dancer maneuvers his stick, the way the drummer holds his tiny sticks in preparation for striking the drum, and the way the artist has placed the banjoist's fingers on the strings to produce the desired sounds.

A second important depiction of African-American culture in the late eighteenth century is Samuel Jennings's allegorical work "Liberty Displaying the Arts and Sciences" (fig. 10), commissioned by the Free Library Company of Philadelphia and completed in 1792. The painting almost literally divides itself into two parts: in the foreground the Goddess of Liberty, surrounded by symbols of literature, sciences, and the arts, holds out books to a family of ex-slaves, who kneel in gratitude before her. And in the middle ground a larger group of ex-slaves, expressing their happiness in a different manner, form a gathering independent of the main group (fig. 11; for convenience of discussion this detail of the painting has been enlarged).

FIGURE 10. Samuel Jennings. "Liberty Displaying the Arts and Sciences." 1792. Oil on canvas. 60¼ × 73⅛ in. Library Company of Philadelphia. Philadelphia, Pennsylvania.

FIGURE 11.   Samuel Jennings. Detail from "Liberty Displaying the Arts and Sciences." 1792. Oil on canvas. Library Company of Philadelphia. Philadelphia, Pennsylvania.

   In several respects the action taking place in the second group is similar to that in "The Old Plantation." The artist has given the ex-slaves of the second group their own miniature social world, which excludes whites, allowing them the opportunity to celebrate their emancipation in their own way. Three adults are shown dancing, in this instance around a Liberty Pole, accompanied by two music-makers and supported by the singing of other figures seated on the ground just ouside the circle of dancers. As in "The Old Plantation," the figures wear American-style attire but dance and make music in African style.

A woman dances the scarf dance, the banjoist plays a long-neck gourd-banjo, and a young boy provides percussive effects by beating on a stick. Were the figures in this scene dressed in African garb, the scene could easily be accepted as representing an African event.

It is unlikely that Jennings intended this abolitionist work to be a genre painting. He gives little attention to depicting this as a scene from the everyday lives of the newly freed slaves but, rather, seems to portray them as symbolic of the African-American experience, suggesting the position they hold in American society at the beginning of a new era and the direction in which they will move into the future. Already, the white artist perceives them as carriers of a distinctive culture, which amalgamates European and African elements, whether developing in the South, as in "The Old Plantation," or above the Mason-Dixon line, as in "Liberty Displaying the Arts and Sciences."

There is yet one other representation of slave culture that survives from the early nineteenth century, a painting entitled "The Banjo Man" (fig. 12, artist and date unknown), which is associated with Williamsburg, Virginia.[10] Reputedly, the painting depicts the celebrated slave fiddler Sy Gilliat (d. 1820), also known as Simon, Simeon, or Cyrus, who played for society balls for many years, at first in Williamsburg during the period between 1740 and 1790, then in Richmond, Virginia, from 1790 until 1820. No proof has been advanced, however, that the banjo player in the painting and the legendary slave fiddler Gilliat were one and the same person.

Despite its anecdotal elements, this painting can hardly be regarded as suggestive of the banjoist's everyday lifestyle, for he is shown not as the determinant of his own actions in this scene but as a servant carrying out the will of his master. Yet, the scene is of value for its references to performance practice of the time, particularly the use of the banjo as a dance instrument.

The three paintings discussed above represent a transitional period for African-American culture in the United States. Generally rejected for entrance into the sociocultural worlds of their slave masters, they attempted to create their own worlds in their new habitat, holding on to the old customs as long as possible, if we accept the evidence of the dance and music pictorial record, which is complemented by contemporary literary evidence of the period. The same kinds of instruments described by the white explorers in West Africa are found among the peoples of the African diaspora, and the same kinds of performance practice—instrumental, vocal, and dance—are observed.

Memories of the Colonial Past

No other genre paintings produced in colonial times have come down to us that show African-Americans in their own private universe, such as is represented in the late-eighteenth-century painting "The Old Plantation." Throughout the

FIGURE 12. "The Banjo Man" (also known as "Cy or Sy Gilliat, Negro Banjo Player"). c.1810. Oil on canvas. Valentine Museum. Richmond, Virginia.

nineteenth century, however, writers turned to graphic artists for assistance in exploring the colonial past, commissioning them to produce illustrations for local histories, romances, travelogues, and other literary forms. Newspapers and journals also recruited artists to prepare illustrations for news features, to accompany reporters in gathering news stories, and, later, to use their sketches as bases for transformation into wood engravings, which were published in such illustrated periodicals as *Harper's New Monthly Magazine* and the *Century Magazine*.

Although no authentic genre paintings of slave life in the colonial period have survived (if they ever existed), we do have six images that purport to represent aspects of colonial African-American culture, of which one appeared in 1860 (fig. 14), two were published in 1876 (figs. 16 and 18), and the other three in the 1890s (figs. 13, 15, and 17). All the illustrations are realistic, that is, they appear to be based on historical facts rather than the invention of some writer's fanciful imagination, as in much of the fiction that poured from the presses in the nineteenth century. Moreover, the pictures presumably represent real people going about their daily tasks as demanded by the social circumstances under which they lived. Consequently, the pictures can be accepted as depicting some aspect of slavery in the eighteenth century despite the fact that the artists were not eyewitnesses to the scenes they depict.

Artist Howard Helmick contributes two representations of slave cultural activity in colonial Maryland, one showing a number of slaves enjoying themselves on a social occasion, "The Juba Dance" (fig. 17), and the other depicting a gathering at a funeral, "The Burial of a Family Servant" (fig. 15). In "The Juba Dance," the social scene, which takes place at night in a tavern or a similar kind of public room, focuses on the dancing of an adolescent, who is closely watched by friends and other customers in the room. Depicted in an extravagant position with head tucked in his shoulders, his body bends almost to his waist, one hand is lifted in the air, and with bent knees and feet bare, he leaps high, jumping from one foot to the other. Actually, this is a couple dance, for a lifted bare foot and an outstretched hand appear opposite the dancer, but the remainder of the person is cut off by the right edge of the picture. People smile at the dancer, one young woman decorously claps her hands in time to the music, and two men lift their hands high, one of them with the obvious intent to produce a loud bang when his left hand falls into his right hand at waist level.

Although the dancer is the focus of attention for the gathered company, Helmick clearly intends that the viewer take account of the fiddler, who sits on a stool in the near-center foreground of the picture, looking out into space as if he were playing for his own enjoyment rather than providing music for the dancing. By the way he has tucked the violin under his chin just so, and poised his bowing arm for a sharp downbow on the next beat, balancing his feet

FIGURE 13. H. P. Arms. "An 'Election Parade' of a Negro Governor." Wash drawing. Published in "Negro Slavery in Connecticut," by Frederick Calvin Norton. *Connecticut Magazine* 5 (1899).

against the rungs of the stool, he gives every appearance of being an experienced fiddler-accompanist, who knows he is producing good music.

And the Juba dance alluded to in the picture's title? Juba, we know from literature of the period, was one of those slave dances with an African prototype, but it is not known at what point in time the dance made its appearance in colonial North America. The word does not appear in colonial writings, although there are eighteenth-century references to a "Negro jig," which might be the same dance with a different name. Modern dance historians, who trace the American Juba dance back to the African *Djouba* or the West Indian *Jumba* or *Majumba*, describe it as "a competitive dance of skill."[11] In his visual description, our artist obviously has caught the essence of the African-American Juba dance and, as well, the warmth of the camaraderie existing among the slaves, despite his not having been an eyewitness to the scene.

"The Burial of a Family Servant" (fig. 15) makes oblique reference to what would become the dominant theme of African-American culture watchers in the nineteenth century, and that is, the religiosity of the slaves—"oblique" because in the antebellum era to come, the slaves generally would take charge of their own burial services, whereas here the artist pictures the slaveholder (or a local clergyman) as conducting the burial service. It was not uncommon, however, for whites to preside over funeral services for their slaves. Though the artist has chosen to capture a moment when the slaveholder was reading from the Scriptures, we know from literary sources that hymn singing was the most important element of the worship service for the black mourners.

Slave Festivities in the North

We have already noted that despite the oppressive bonds of slavery, black folk found ways to continue some of their traditional African practices in the English colonies, of which the most spectacular were the slave festivals that took place periodically wherever there were large concentrations of slaves. Although they came from a variety of nations, the slaves shared in common enough music and dance traditions to enable them to communicate with each other through the performing arts despite their different languages and customs.

As previously mentioned, Pinkster, which dated from a time when slavery flourished in the middle colonies, was one of the earliest of these festivals. Originally a principal Dutch holiday associated with the observance of Pentecost, by the eighteenth century the slaves had taken over the fete, making it their very own. It was noted for its African dancing and music-making that attracted large crowds of white and black spectators. The celebration was particularly vivacious at Albany, New York: there the slave dancers had their special dancing grounds on Pinkster Hill, and their own reigning monarch, King

Charley of Angola (c.1699–1824), who "called" the dancing and also reportedly played the master drums and other instruments for a period of over one hundred years.

Several descriptions of the Pinkster festivals are extant, one of the earliest ones a lengthy "Pinkster Ode/For the Year 1803/Most Respectfully Dedicated to/Carolus Africanus, Rex . . . ," which is credited to one Absalom Aimwell, Esq. Written in the best classical tradition, it addresses those who would join in the celebration

> *Of Pinkster, who presumes to sing,*
> *Must homage pay to Charles the King: . . .*
> *Tho' for a sceptre he was born,*
> *Tho' from his father's kingdom torn,*
> *And doom'd to be a slave; still he*
> *Retains his native majesty.*
>
> *Now hark! the Banjo, rub a dub,*
> *Like a washer-woman's tub;*
> *Now hear the drum, 'tis rolling now,*
> *Row de dow, row de dow.*
> *The pipe and tabor, flute and fife,*
> *Shall wake the dullest soul to life,*
> *All beneath the shady tree*
> *There they hold the jubilee.*
> *Charles, the King, will then advance,*
> *Leading on the Guinea dance,*
> *Moving o'er the flow'ry green,*
> *You'll know him by his graceful mien; . . .*
> *And when you know him, then you'll see*
> *A slave whose soul was always free. . . .*[12]

Other sources report on the African instruments, the excitement of the crowds, and the dancing, "[which] had its peculiarities, as well as everything else connected with this august celebration. It consisted chiefly of couples joining in the performances at varying times [fig. 14], and continuing it with their utmost energy until extreme fatigue or weariness compelled them to retire and give space to a less exhausted set. . . ."[13]

From about 1750 until as late as the 1850s in some places, blacks in New England celebrated a holiday known as 'Lection Day, which coincided with the observance of Election Day by the white population. Depending upon the town or village, the holiday was celebrated in May or June; in most places the slave elected to "rule" his people for the coming year was called a "governor," but in some places he was a "king." Slaveholders allowed their slaves time off to

FIGURE 14. Felix Octavius Carr Darley. [Pinkster Dancers.] Pen and ink. Published in *Satanstoe: Or, the Littlepage Manuscripts,* by James Fenimore Cooper. New York: Townsend and Company, 1860.

elect their rulers, hold parades, and celebrate afterward with wrestling, games, singing, and dancing (except in Puritan strongholds).

Processions were an especially attractive feature of the festivals: in some places, black troupes numbering as many as one hundred would engage in the marching—some two by two on foot, some mounted on horseback—with drums beating, colors flying, and the music of fifes, fiddles, clarionets, and "every sonorous metal that could be found uttering a martial sound."[14] White spectators of the parades in Newport, Rhode Island, were struck by the singing: "every voice upon its highest key, in all the various languages of Africa, mixed with broken and ludicrous English, filled the air, accompanied with the music of the fiddle, tambourine, banjo, and drum."[15]

"An 'Election Parade' of a Negro Governor" (fig. 13) represents the annual procession that took place in colonial Connecticut. The "governor," sitting haughty and imperious on his horse, with eyes straight ahead as if looking into the future, occupies the center foreground of the image, followed by members of his court. Spectators dressed in their finest line the street, the children scrambling to keep up with the parade.

What comes to the mind of the king? Does he have racial memories of African kings leading processions at the Annual Custom in Dahomey or the Yam Custom in Ashanti, accompanied by their "tributaries and captains . . .

FIGURE 15. Howard Helmick. "The Burial of a Family Servant." Wood engraving by C. W. Chadwick. Published in "Old Maryland Homes and Ways," by John Williamson Palmer. *Century Magazine* 49 (1894).

FIGURE 16. Edwin Austin Abbey. "Slaves' Quarters in the Cellar of the Old Knicker-bocker Mansion." Wood engraving by French. Published in "The Knickerbockers of New York Two Centuries Ago," by Egbert T. Viele. *Harper's New Monthly Magazine* 54 (1876).

surrounded by attendants of every description"? Does he recall "the sound of more than a hundred bands burst[ing] at once with the peculiar airs of their several chiefs; the horns flourishing their defiances, with the beatings of innumerable drums and metal instruments"?[16]

Domesticity and Music-Making

In depicting the social activities of the African-American family, artists generally drew on the same pictorial conventions they used in depicting white families, but of course transferred the settings to slave environments. The domestic

FIGURE 17. Howard Helmick. "The Juba Dance." Wood engraving by E. H. Del' Orme. Published in "Old Maryland Homes and Ways," by John Williamson Palmer. *Century Magazine* 49 (1894).

scene typically shows the family gathered for relaxation in its slave living quarters at the end of the workday or, in warm-weather climates, assembled in front of the slave cabin. Invariably, the stock images include on center stage a male fiddler or banjoist, the master music-maker who entertains the group; one or two boys dancing in the foreground; and an indeterminate number of spectators in the middle ground and background, members of the extended family and friends, who express appreciation variously, ranging from outbursts of wild enthusiasm to hand-clapping with restrained decorum.

Any number of variations on this theme may be found in the pictorial record, among the most common, the scenario where the onlookers sing along with the entertainer and/or a male member provides an accompaniment by "pattin' Juba." (We will return to discussion of pattin'.) Another version favored by artists shows a younger member of the family, perhaps a talented adolescent,

FIGURE 18. "In Ole Virginny." Wood engraving. Published in "Virginia in the Revolution," by John Esten Cooke. *Harper's New Monthly Magazine* 53 (1876).

providing the entertainment, or perhaps it is a visitor who contributes to the merrymaking. Through the years many artists found this theme to be appealing—though sometimes it bordered on the stereotypical—and any number of surviving paintings and prints successfully exploit its formulas and conventions.

Two examples of the domestic-images theme are included in our group of colonial scenes. The print "In Ole Virginny" (fig. 18) shows a slave family choosing to spend its leisure time in making music and dancing, this taking place during the colonial era, judging from the colonial-style dress of the figures, on a plantation in the colony of Virginia, judging from the title of the picture. Edwin Abbey's print "Slaves' Quarters in the Cellar of the Old Knickerbocker Mansion" (fig. 16) offers more particulars than the "Virginny" print, enabling the viewer to situate the figures in time-and-place context, to appreciate the social circumstances of the family gathering, and to gain some insight into performance practice regarding the dancing, fiddling, and pattin'.

Given the center foreground position, the boy dancer is surrounded by members of his immediate family in the left middle ground and by the fiddler on the right, all of whom exhibit great pride in his skills, as well as appreciation for the entertainment he provides. One of the adult males appears on the verge of clapping his hands, but it is no ordinary hand-clapping: he bends forward from the waist, his thighs thrust outward and knees bent backward. His next move will be to slap his thighs, then repeat his actions, perhaps varying them somewhat. This complex hand-clapping, thigh-slapping movement is called "pattin' Juba" (or Juber); its primary function is to accompany the dance.

Hand-clapping as an essential element of African-style dancing was remarked in the earliest writings of the explorers in Africa and continued to provoke discussion through the years. It is not known when the elaborate hand-clapping practice identified as "pattin' Juba" began to attract attention in the mainland colonies; no references have yet been found in eighteenth-century sources, but by the 1830s, writers were using the term so freely that they did not feel it necessary to explain it to their readers, thus suggesting that "pattin' Juba" had been around a long time.

There were many ways to "pat," depending upon the patter. Visiting a Maryland plantation in 1832, a young lawyer, James Hungerford, observed that the slave Ike patted by "singing the words of a jig in a monotonous tone of voice, beating time meanwhile with his hands alternately against each other and against his body."[17] On the other hand, Clotilda, regarded as the best patter on the plantation, recited her "verses in a shrill sing-song voice," keeping time to the measure, as Ike had done, by beating her hands sometimes against her sides, and patting the ground with her feet. And a visitor to a Virginia plantation in the 1830s saw slaves dancing a jig around "two sticks lying crosswise upon the ground, alternately slapping their thighs and throwing up their elbows to the time of the music."[18]

Reminiscences of Africa in Old New Orleans

In the eighteenth and early nineteenth centuries, New Orleans, Louisiana, was arguably the most exotic city on the mainland, largely because of its mix of French, Spanish, and African cultures—and, after the purchase of the Louisiana Territory in 1803—that of the Americans. Among the obligatory sights for tourists was the dancing of the slaves on Sunday afternoons in an area of the city that came to be known as Congo Square or Place Congo. While the origin of this tradition is obscure, references to it in books published by travelers and local historians began to appear in the early 1700s. French planter Antoine Simon le Page du Pratz, for example, who lived in Louisiana from c. 1718 to 1735, notes in his *History of Louisiana* that on Sundays the slaves danced the Calinda in groups as large as three or four hundred, and he was only among the earliest of a long succession of writers who were moved to comment on the African dancing that occurred in the Place Congo.[19]

Most notable of these writers was the architect Benjamin Latrobe, who on February 21, 1819, wrote a detailed account in his diary of the events associated with the slave dancing in Place Congo and included sketches of some of the musical instruments.[20] Certainly the most colorful of the reporters was George Washington Cable, who in 1886 published two articles, "The Dance in Place Congo" and "Creole Slave Songs," for which he engaged artist Edward Windsor Kemble to make twenty illustrations. Six of them have musical subject matter. Since Kemble himself did not see the dancing in Place Congo (which was banned by city authorities in the 1840s), he would have had to rely on the memories of others or on published sources, some of which were written by writers who themselves had not been eyewitnesses to the Place Congo dancing. Cable of course was among the latter. But in his articles he "borrowed" extensively from Moreau de Saint-Mery and Latrobe, among others, and so successfully evoked the scenes of the Place Congo dancing that artist Kemble was able to draw the commissioned pictures by transforming Cable's prose descriptions into visual images. Three examples presented here are "The Bamboula" (figs. 19 and 20), "The Love Song" (fig. 21), and "The Voodoo Dance" (fig. 22).

FIGURE 19. Edward Windsor Kemble. "The Bamboula." 1885. Pen and ink. Published in "The Dance in Place Congo," by George W. Cable. *Century Magazine* 31 (1886).

FIGURE 20. Edward Windsor Kemble.
Detail from "The Bamboula." Pen and ink.
Published in "The Dance in Place Congo,"
by George W. Cable. *Century Magazine* 31
(1886).

FIGURE 21. Edward Windsor Kemble.
"The Love Song." Pen and ink. Published
in "The Dance in Place Congo," by George
W. Cable. *Century Magazine* 31 (1886).

In *Dance*, Moreau de Saint-Mery describes the African-style dance called the
Bamboula as he saw it in 1796 when traveling in the Caribbean and Louisiana:

> When they are ready to dance, the negroes take two drums, that is, two
> barrels of unequal length; one end of each remains open and the other is
> covered by a tightly stretched lamb skin. These drums (the shorter of
> which is called the Bamboula because often it is fashioned from a large
> bamboo which has been dug out) sound out as they are given fist and fin-
> ger knocks by each player bent over his drum. . . . These monotonous
> and low notes are accompanied by a number of Callebasses, containing
> gravel which is agitated by means of a long handle. The Banzas, a sort of

FIGURE 22. Edward Windsor Kemble. "The Voodoo Dance." 1885. Pen and ink. Published in "Creole Slave Songs," by George W. Cable. *Century Magazine* 31 (1886).

primitive guitar with four strings, joins the concert, the timing being controlled by hand-clapping negresses standing in a large circle; the group forms a kind of chorus, replying to one or two principal singers whose remarkable voices repeat or improvise on a song. A dancer and his partner, or a number of pairs of dancers, advance to the center and begin to dance, always as couples.[21]

Cable recounts this description in his articles of 1886, almost a hundred years later, embroidering it profusely and placing it in the context of the original setting. He treats the other two New Orleans scenes (figs. 21 and 22) in a similar fashion.

Using as a setting for his Bamboula image a "flat, grassy plain" with the skyline of New Orleans in the background, artist Kemble has divided his picture into two parts; the left side is dominated by the dancers and the right, by the musical forces (see fig. 20 for an enlargement of the image). Four drummers sit astride small drums on the first row; one sits beside a larger drum on the second row; and a man on the third row waves a callebasse. Surrounding the whole are hundreds of slaves in circle formation, clapping their hands and singing with tremendous vigor, judging by their widely open mouths and their body stances. The viewer is to assume, as Moreau (as well as many other writers) states, that one or two voices sing the verses, and the crowds come in on the choruses. The scene is a direct throwback to Africa.

Two images of a voodoo ceremony are included in our collection, Kemble's "The Voodoo Dance" (fig. 22) and the anonymous "The Voudou Meeting in the Old Brick-Yard" (fig. 23). While there seem to be no extant reports by eyewitnesses on the voodoo rites of colonial New Orleans, references to these rites are found in a number of publications, and it appears that some nineteenth-century writers published sensational accounts that distorted the facts. Among the more reliable, if overly colorful, descriptions is that of historian Henry Castellanos, who devoted a large part of his book *New Orleans As It Was . . .* (1895) to discussion of voodoo.

> Who has not heard, in connection with the local history of New Orleans, of that mysterious and religious sect of fanatics, imported from the jungles of Africa and implanted in our midst, so well known under the appellation of *Voudous?* St. John's Day—the 24th of June—is the day consecrated by them to their peculiar idolatry. . . . [Castellanos errs; the traditional date was St. John's Eve, June 23rd]. According to the Africans of the Arada nation, who claim to have preserved unsullied the faith and ceremonies of their religion, the word "Voudou" signifies an all-powerful and supernatural Being, from whom all events derive their origin. And what or who is that Being? A serpent, a harmless snake, under whose auspices these religionists gather.[22]

Castellanos elaborates further on the functions of the two ministers of the God-Serpent (Dambala), who claim to act under its bidding, and are called King and Queen or, at other times, Master and Mistress, and sometimes the affectionate names Papa and Mama. The voodoo ceremony includes "the adoration of his Snakeship," oracle pronouncements from the lips of the Queen, initiation of candidates, and spirit possession.

The voodoo scenes feature the dancing both of individuals, probably initiates (fig. 22), and of a large group (fig. 23). Motifs associated with voodoo, African-American, and Christian European rituals are much in evidence, such as the use of candles for initiation purposes, the singing and hand-clapping of the spectators, and the emphasis on circle formations. Though Kemble does not depict stringed instruments in the musical forces for the Bamboula, he does put African instruments, a three-string gourd-fiddle and two drums, in the voodoo orchestra.

"The Voudou Meeting" (fig. 23) is not a dance but rather a voodoo ceremony, which was not open to the public. The scene depicts chaos, with its whirling figures dancing in the darkness, some fallen on the ground and some waving their hands in the air. A bright fire in the left background of the picture throws the scene into sharp contrasts, which reveals the source of the music for the dancing —a banjoist in the top center of the picture, and a player on the tam-tam (a long drum) to the left. Both instruments are of African origin.

FIGURE 23. "The Voudou Meeting in the Old Brick-Yard." Wood engraving. Published in *Metropolitan Life Unveiled* . . . , by James W. Buel. St. Louis: Historical Publishing Company, 1882.

Notes

1. Poesch, *Art* 173–74.
2. In some of the pictures, the banjo is given three strings; in other pictures, there are four strings. Frequently, an additional short string is depicted, thus producing the four- or five-string instrument.
3. Moreau, *Dance,* 55, 61.
4. "Musical Gleanings [1826]," 94.
5. Clapperton, *Narrative,* 2:402.
6. Jobson, *Golden Trade,* 106.
7. Bosman, *New Description;* Clapperton, *Journal,* 89.
8. Smyth, *Tour,* 43.
9. Poesch, *Art,* 174. Poesch observes that it was common in the early nineteenth century to use paintings or drawings as a way of preserving records of important events.
10. See further discussion about "The Banjo Man" in Mordecai, *Richmond,* 178, 310.
11. Emery, *Black Dance,* 96. Emery also quotes from Katherine Dunham, "The Negro Dance," in *The Negro Caravan* (New York: Dryden Press, 1941), 997–98; and William B. Smith, "The Persimmon Tree and the Beer Dance" in *Farmer's Register* (April 1838): 58–61.
12. Aimwell, "Pinkster Ode."

13. James Eights, "Pinkster Festivities," in Joel Munsell, ed., *Collections on the History of Albany* (Albany, New York: J. Munsell, 1865) 2:326. A reprint of this article is available in Southern, *Readings.*

14. Stuart, *Hartford,* 39.

15. Platt, "Negro Governors," 324.

16. The quoted material in this passage is from Bowdich, *Mission,* 33. Many of Bowdich's passages about music are reprinted in Southern, *Readings.*

17. The quotations in this passage are from Hungerford, *Old Plantation,* 190–99. There is a striking similarity between this song and dance practice called "pattin' Juba" and the twentieth-century song and dance "rapping."

18. Kennedy, *Swallow Barn,* 1:160.

19. Le Page du Pratz, *History,* 31.

20. Latrobe, *Journal,* 49–51.

21. Moreau, *Dance,* 52–55.

22. Castellanos, *New Orleans,* 90–91, 94.

PART II

THE
ANTEBELLUM
ERA

Church and Ritual

In the antebellum period a relatively large number of genre paintings and drawings were produced, which, taken together, give an extensive pictorial overview of African-American folk culture during this period, particularly in the decade leading directly up to the Civil War and Emancipation. Classified on the basis of subject matter, the artworks fall into discrete classes, depicting religious activities, social gatherings, laborers at work and at play, processions of various kinds, and social interaction between and among individuals. To understand the images shown in antebellum artworks we must consider the details of the sociocultural world in which African-Americans lived, and construct a historical framework that will accommodate the details.

Missionaries to the Slaves

The first colonial institution to impact on the Africans newly arrived in the colonies was the Protestant Church.[1] Early in the eighteenth century the Church of England set as one of its major goals the converting of the so-called heathens of the New World, the Indians and Africans, to Christianity. Through its Society for the Propagation of the Gospel in Foreign Parts (founded in 1701) and its Associates of Doctor Bray (established in 1723), the Church sent over missionaries to minister to the slaves. The story of how British missionaries Christianized a small number of the pagan Africans in the colonies, gave them religious instruction, and, knowingly or unknowingly, prepared them to work among their own people is deeply moving, but beyond the confines of the present discussion.

With the outbreak of the Revolutionary War, the Anglican missionaries of course were forced to leave the colonies, but others who had entered the field—particularly the Methodists, Baptists, and Presbyterians—undertook to carry on the important work begun by the pioneering British. It was an immense, long-lasting enterprise, which sustained itself through the rise of the independent black church in the late eighteenth century, the flourishing of the plantation mission in the mid-nineteenth century, and the establishment of schools and other missions for the contrabands, the freedmen, and their descendants well into the twentieth century.

We are not sure just when black Christians began to organize autonomous congregations under the leadership of their own preachers. Documentary evidence for blacks holding religious meetings away from the supervision of their masters dates as far back as the 1690s, and undoubtedly it was under such circumstances that black Christian leadership slowly developed over the years.[2] By the 1770s, independent Baptist groups had begun to surface in the South, first among them, George Leile's congregation c.1774 at Silver Bluff, South Carolina, and a few years later, in 1788, Andrew Bryan's First African Baptist Church at Savannah, Georgia. The latter is regarded as the first permanent black congregation in the nation.

Beginning in the 1780s and continuing through the early nineteenth century, black Protestants in the North withdrew from their white mother churches to form their own congregations: the Methodists in Baltimore (1787), Philadelphia (1787), and New York (1795); the Baptists in Boston (1805), New York (1808), and Philadelphia (1808); the Presbyterians in Philadelphia (1807); and the Episcopalians in Philadelphia (1794) and New York (1818).

From the white Methodist Episcopal Church came the first autonomous black denominations in history. Under the dynamic leadership of the ex-slave preacher Richard Allen (1760–1831), the African Methodist Episcopal Mother Bethel Church at Philadelphia (hereafter AME) was organized in 1794 and chartered in 1816 after more than a decade of contention with Old St. George's Methodist Church, its parent church. In New York, black Methodists formed their own congregation in 1796 as the African Methodist Episcopal Zion Church (hereafter AMEZ), which received its charter in 1821. The Union African Methodist Episcopal Church of Wilmington, Delaware, formed in 1805, was incorporated in 1813.

Although the black self-governing churches were established primarily above the Mason-Dixon Line, independent congregations also could be found in the South in such urban areas as Charleston, South Carolina, Richmond, Virginia, and New Orleans, Louisiana. Notwithstanding the activities of the newly established black churches, the religious needs of most of the nation's

slave population—which numbered almost four million by 1860 (3,953,760)—
were generally neglected, though in some places itinerant white clergymen or
resident slave exhorters were permitted to preach to the slaves. After the Den-
mark Vesey rebellion in 1821, however, and the Nat Turner insurrection in 1831,
the Southern states passed ever more stringent laws to keep their slave popu-
lations under control, and they reinforced more strictly those laws that had
been passed in earlier times. These laws, the so-called Black Codes, prohibited
or restricted whites and free blacks from teaching slaves to read, and blacks
from preaching or gathering in sizable numbers for any purpose unless
"respectable whites" were present (the number of whites required varied from
state to state).

Antebellum writers—particularly the clergymen, European travelers, ex-
slaves, and journalists upon whom we depend for eyewitness documentation—found the black folk church to be exotic at the least and, in some
respects, overwhelming. After visiting the urban churches and the praise cabins set aside for worship services on the plantations, they often came away feeling inadequate to describe what they had experienced. They reported on the
fiery oratory of the preacher; the exclamatory responses of the congregation to
his preachments in a call-and-response exchange; the hand-clapping and foot-
stomping; the moaning, shouting, shrieking, and jumping up and down; and
the singing of impromptu religious songs (improvised by the church members) along with the prescribed Protestant hymns. But always there seemed to
be a missing element, an indefinable quality, that prevented white writers from
comprehending the full significance of African-American religious practices.
As will become evident, the visual records discussed here provide insight into
how an African-American expressive culture developed in the nineteenth century, and, in many instances, the pictures complement written documents,
thus adding new dimensions to the literature.

Of the sixty-nine works of art that constitute our antebellum collection,
eleven present religious subject matter (figs. 24–34), thirty-one offer music
and dance subject matter in reference to the plantation (figs. 35–65), seventeen
have to do with urban music and the context in which it occurred (figs. 66–82),
and ten depict musical subject matter related to the Civil War (figs. 83–92).
Few of the artworks date from the first half of the nineteenth century; for the
most part, they were produced in the 1850s and early 1860s, a time when Americans were becoming increasingly involved with the nation's bitter controversy
over slavery and increasingly concerned about the place of African-Americans
in the fast-changing social world. The public expressed an interest in learning
more about the troublesome black folk who stood at the center of the controversy, and artists and writers responded to the demand.

Worship Services in Urban Churches

We are indebted to the Russian diplomat Pavel Petrovich Svin'in for the earliest pictorial and literary reports on African-American religious practices. Secretary during the years 1811 to 1813 to the Russian Consul General in Philadelphia, Svin'in took frequent sightseeing trips up and down the eastern seaboard during his stay of twenty months in the city and, fascinated by the American people and their lifestyles, kept a record of his experiences in both notebooks and sketchbooks. Returning home with a portfolio of fifty-two watercolors and enough notes to permit him to write a travelogue, he published *A Picturesque Voyage through North America* in 1815.[3]

Svin'in's portrayal of a black-church religious scene, "Negro Methodists Holding a Meeting in Philadelphia" (fig. 24, c.1812), is the earliest extant representation of the black-church genre, based on all evidence. The painting shows an indeterminant number of men and women, and one or two children, gathered in front of a building, presumably their meeting house, where they sing, howl, dance like whirling dervishes, and fall prostrate on the ground. In the

FIGURE 24. Pavel (Paul) Petrovich Svin'in. "Negro Methodists Holding a Meeting in Philadelphia" (also known as "Frenzied Negro Methodists Holding a Religious Meeting in a Philadelphia Alley"). c.1812. Watercolor on paper. 6⅝ × 10 in. Metropolitan Museum of Art, Rogers Fund, 1942 (acc. no. 42.95.19). New York, New York.

upper center of the picture stands what appears to be a clergyman with arms outstretched and a worried look on his face, suggesting he fears things may have gotten out of hand. But he makes no effort to bring order out of the chaos, for the worshipers genuinely seem to be possessed by the Holy Spirit. The fact that the action occurs outside the doors of the church, away from the control of the minister, indicates this is probably an informal service—taking place after the formal service on Sunday or after the weekly prayer meeting.

It should be remembered that though most of the worshipers pictured here are freedmen, they undoubtedly were born into slavery (Pennsylvania began to emancipate its slaves in 1780) and consequently appreciate the reality that freedom has brought them the privilege of worshiping as they please. Throughout the nineteenth century and into the twentieth, black and white clergymen would try to purge black folk church rituals of their African elements, particularly the holy dance and spirit possession, but to no avail.

In all likelihood, Svin'in's watercolor is a visual record of his visit to one of Philadelphia's African Methodist churches. His alternative title for this scene, which labeled the black Methodists as "frenzied," does not necessarily signify that only black Methodists indulged in extravagant religious practices during this period, but their skin color and religious exuberance apparently make them more "picturesque" to Svin'in than the white Methodist congregations. There is no reason to doubt that Svin'in painted this scene from life, no matter how fanciful it seems. Indeed, it is probable that the worshipers belong to Richard Allen's church (see p. 44), for there were only two black Methodist churches in Philadelphia in 1812, Allen's Bethel AME Church and the Zoar Methodist Church, and Zoar was still under governance of the white mother church, Old St. George's, at that time.

Svin'in writes in great detail about his visit, describing the service with considerable disparagement, especially as compared to the dignity and splendor of the worship services of his Orthodox church. Noting that the preacher began his sermon in a "fluent, hoarse voice" and "bombastic style," Svin'in relates how the preacher played upon the emotions of the congregation, building up the tension until there could be heard "the groans of the penitent and the cries and exclamations of the possessed." In describing the singing, he observes: "At the end of every psalm the entire congregation, men and women alike, sang verses in a loud shrill monotone. . . . When the preacher ceased reading, all turned toward the door, fell on their knees, bowed their heads to the ground, and set up an agonizing, heart-rending moaning."[4]

Despite the patronizing tone of Svin'in's words, they have historical significance as the earliest pictorial and literary records of the black congregation that constituted the core of the world's first black denomination, the AME Church, and cultural significance as the first portrayal in history of an informal religious service of black Christians. Moreover, these reports offer eyewitness testimony about church-music performance practice as well as insight into the religious practices of the minister and his congregation, and thus the accuracy of Svin'in's reports is corroborated by contemporary sources.

Though few in number in the early nineteenth century, urban black churches were tourist attractions for traveling Europeans and many of them, like Svin'in, included descriptions of the worship services they had attended in the books they published when they returned home. One of the most celebrated of the travelers, Swedish novelist Frederika Bremer (1801–1865), visited two of Cincinnati's African-American churches in November 1850 and recorded the experience in her diary, later published in *Homes of the New World: Impressions of America* (1853).

In the forenoon, Bremer visited the "negro Baptist church belonging to the Episcopal [*sic*] creed," where she noticed that the few worshipers present were members of the Negro aristocracy; the minister was "a fair mulatto . . . of very good intellect and conversational power"; and "the mode of conducting the divine service was quiet, very proper, and a little tedious." That afternoon found her in the African Methodist Church, where she encountered, in contrast to her morning experience, "African ardor and African life":

> The church was full to overflowing, and the congregation sang their own hymns. The singing ascended and poured forth like a melodious torrent, and the heads, feet, and elbows of the congregation moved all in unison with it, amid evident enchantment and delight in the singing, which was in itself exquisitely pure and full of melodious life. . . . After the singing of the hymns, which was not led by any organ or musical instrument, whatever, but which arose like burning melodious sighs from the breasts of the congregation, the preacher mounted the pulpit. He was a very black negro, young, with a very retreating forehead . . . not at all good-looking. But when he began to speak, the congregation hung upon his words, and I could not help but admire his flowing eloquence. . . .[5]

Bremer continues by giving a vivid account of the sermon and the worshipers' increasingly emotional responses to the preaching. Finally, she concludes, "The whole congregation was for several minutes like a stormy sea. The preacher's address had been a rushing tempest of national eloquence."[6]

By a fortunate coincidence, we have discovered an engraving of a black church in Cincinnati that corresponds precisely to Bremer's report on her visit to the AME Church in 1850 (fig. 25). The anonymous artist, who depicts a formal worship service in progress in his "Meeting in the African Church, Cincinnati, Ohio," employs the conventional motifs and images associated with the black folk church. The preacher—judging by his body position, outstretched arms, and serious mien—is approaching the high point of his sermon, and the worshipers are responding to his rising voice and increasing emotionalism with varying degrees of spiritedness. We know from literary sources how they

FIGURE 25. "Meeting in the African Church, Cincinnati, Ohio." c.1853. Wood engraving. Courtesy of the Library of Congress. Washington, D.C.

respond: some cry out "Amen," "Yes, Yes," "Oh, glory," and the like; others pray aloud in a kind of moaning counterpoint to the preaching, which by this point in the sermon is more chanting than speaking. One or two wave their hands in the air. What appears to be the mourner's bench just below the altar is filled, but some nevertheless move forward in search of a place to sit on it, or near it. To the viewer the scene might appear chaotic, but based on available evidence, it depicts a realistic moment in the religious service of a free, urban, black congregation in the early 1850s.

Worship in a Plantation Church

A third religious picture presents stark contrast to the scenes discussed above, though it employs the same pictorial conventions and makes reference to the same theme. "Family Worship in [*sic*] a Plantation in South Carolina" (fig. 26) offers a glimpse into the religious practices of a slave congregation, as distinguished from a congregation of freedmen. As required by law, "respectable

FIGURE 26. Thomas Nast. "Family Worship in [*sic*] a Plantation in South Carolina." Wood engraving by Mason Jackson. Published in "Slaves at Worship on a Plantation in South Carolina." *Illustrated London News* 43 (1863).

whites" are present—in this instance, the slaveholder and his family. Aside from the slave master and two men who have dozed off, all present have their eyes glued on the preacher, whose back is to the viewer. He has not yet reached the climax of his sermon: only one hand is uplifted, the other rests on the open Bible, where his fingers follow the text as he talks. His listeners, though engrossed in his message, are subdued.

There is nothing in this scene of tranquility drawn in 1863 to suggest that outside the walls of the "praise cabin" a nation is engaged in a death struggle over the issue of slavery. Nor is there any indication that members of the group are concerned about their status as slaves and slaveholder, or about relations between black and white. Subtly, the picture informs that, war or no war, it is unlikely that political and social conditions will change on the plantations of the South. Although the black preacher stands tall in the center of the picture, towering over the heads of his listeners, and symbolically appears even taller because of his uplifted left arm, the white slave master clearly is the central figure in terms of authority and power. The very "whiteness" of his presence—his

skin color, bald head, white suit—surrounded by the blackness of the worshipers insures that the viewer's attention first goes to the slaveholder before
exploring the contents of the scene, and constantly returns to his image as if
drawn by a magnet.

The "Invisible" Black Church

During the mid-nineteenth century the newly established plantation-mission
movement in the South began to reach out to slaves who, for one reason or
another, did not attend church.[7] Some who lived in urban areas accompanied
their masters to church, where they occupied segregated pews or sat outside
beneath the church windows. In places where the approval of the slaveholders
could be obtained, religious meetings were held in "praise cabins" set aside on
the plantations for that purpose. Although the law demanded that whites be
present at religious meetings, as depicted in the Thomas Nast picture (fig. 26),
there is evidence in the literature, particularly the slave narratives, that in
many places slaves conducted their own meetings in defiance of the law.

The prevalent kind of religious experience for slaves during the antebellum
period, however, was offered by the so-called invisible church. Left to their
own governance, the slaves practiced a Christianity that absorbed African elements, listening and responding to the passionate oratory of their exhorters,
singing their improvised spirituals in addition to the standard Protestant
hymns, dancing the holy dance called "the shout," and welcoming the Holy
Spirit to take possession of their souls. (We will return to discussion of the
shout.) Where the slaveholders disallowed religious activities, the slaves held
secret meetings in the bush, woods, thickets, or ravines, and resorted to various devices to prevent the sounds of worship from reaching the slaveholder's
ears. Regrettably, no pictorial records of these surreptitious meetings seem to
have survived from the antebellum period, but literary sources of the period
are replete with accounts of the "invisible church."

Antebellum Burial Rites

Perhaps no religious activity of antebellum blacks held more fascination for
whites, American as well as European, than the burial rites of black folk, particularly the slaves. Again and again in antebellum writings we find comment
on burial practices that point back to Africa and the elaborate distinctions
between burial rites and funeral ceremonies—the latter might occur days,
weeks, or even months after the burial. In those instances when a service was
conducted at the burial site, the formal funeral that took place later was called
"the second funeral."

Writing in 1856, the Reverend John Dixon Long discusses the slave burial and how it differs from the funeral:

> The death of a slave is considered a mere money loss. Neighbor A says that "Neighbor B has lost a fine slave worth one thousand dollars." The humble body is buried in the negro graveyard, in some obscure part of the plantation. For the slave there is no tombstone. The flowers of memory and affection never bloom over the lonely hillock that marks his resting place. . . . Many an undeveloped poet, orator, and artist lies entombed in such obscure cemeteries throughout the South.
>
> A negro funeral is different from the "burying," and is a unique affair. Several weeks after the burial the funeral is preached; and never was there more frolic at an Irish wake than at these funerals, held frequently in the woods, and sometimes as many as three funerals are preached at once. Unless a colored person is preached, whether he be saint or sinner, there is no peace of mind to his friends.[8]

Five of the six burial/funeral scenes in our antebellum collection (figs. 29–33) depict events that took place in the Deep South during the 1850s and 1860s. George Fuller, represented here by two artworks, bases his oil painting, "Negro Funeral" (fig. 31, 1881), on his sketch of a slave funeral he had seen in March 1858 during his stay in Montgomery, Alabama (fig. 32). He did not construct the oil painting based on the sketch until many years later. It is probable that the John Antrobus painting, "A Plantation Burial" (fig. 33), also was conceived in Montgomery, where Antrobus lived from 1855 to about 1860. Both paintings reflect the artists' concern for meticulous detail in re-creating events they had seen with their own eyes.

Other artists who had not been eyewitnesses to the scenes they depicted also show concern for realistic detail, as in, for example, William Ludlow Sheppard's "An Old-Time Midnight Slave Funeral" (fig. 30) and Arthur Burdett Frost's "A Negro Funeral in Virginia" (fig. 29). All five artworks convey to the viewer the sense of great anguish and desolation associated with the slave burial.

Over time, artists developed a repertory of burial/funeral motifs and themes, which could be drawn upon when necessary to depict this most consecrated of African-American religious services. There was the mournful procession from the slave quarters to the distant gravesite, for example, which might consist of a few members of the family (fig. 29) or of dozens (figs. 31 and 32); the use of a heavily wooded area as the setting, often under midnight skies (figs. 30, 33, and 34); the transport of the coffin by mule-led cart (fig. 29) or by human hands (fig. 30); and the wild, wailing laments of the mourners. Artists of course possessed their own personal repertories of artistic devices and symbols, which they used to particularize further their scenes. Always the preacher is the central figure: he conducts the service with arms outstretched, the slaves gathering around him in varying degrees of attentiveness, and the congregation is composed of children and adults of all ages.

Other frequently used motifs include a group of whites placed peripherally to the main action, in the background or on the right or left sides of the scene, and the men (who may or may not be mourners) offering, or prepared to offer, such services as carrying the coffin, digging the grave, sweeping the grave with pine branches, and lowering the coffin into the grave.

Clergyman Hamilton W. Pierson, writing about his attendance at a slave funeral in the 1840s, is informative for his substantiation of evidence offered by pictorial sources:

> During my stay in the neighborhood, a slave died upon one of the plantations, and I was told that I would have an opportunity of witnessing one of their favorite funerals. In those portions of the South where the plantations were largest, and the slaves the most numerous, they were very fond of burying their dead at night, and as near midnight as possible. In case of a funeral, they assembled in large numbers from adjoining plantations, provided with pine-knots, and pieces of fat pine called lightwood, which when ignited made a blaze compared with which our city torch-light processions are most sorry affairs. When all was in readiness, they lighted these torches, formed into a procession, and marched slowly to the distant grave, singing the most solemn music. Sometimes they sang hymns they had committed to memory, but oftener those more tender and plaintive [songs], composed by themselves. . . .
>
> But to return to this midnight funeral. The appearance of such a procession, winding through the fields and woods, as revealed by their flaming torches, marching slowly to the sound of their wild music, was weird and imposing in the highest degree. . . . This procession was to pass immediately by our door, but, in order to get a fuller view, a small company of us went out a short distance to meet them. We saw them and heard their music in the distance, as they came down a gentle descent, crossed over a small stream, and then marched on some time in silence. As they came near where we stood, we heard their leader announce in the sing-song, chanting style I have already described, the words "When I can read my title clear"; and that long procession, with their flaming fat-pine torches, marched by us with slow and solemn tread, singing that beautiful hymn to the tune of "Ortonville." We followed to the place of burial, listened to their songs and addresses at the grave, and witnessed all the ceremonies to the close.[9]

The Bible and the Importance of Learning to Read

Despite the limited amount of leisure time allowed the slaves and the close restrictions the slavery system placed upon their movement, many of them contrived ways to pursue personal interests. High on the list of priorities for some slaves was learning how to read, and this aspiration was not confined to religious leaders and the highly devout. Take the case of ex-slave Frederick Douglass (c.1817–95), for example, who recounts in his biography how, as a young boy of seven or eight, he first became aware of the importance of literacy. His master's wife had begun to teach him, first the ABCs, then how to spell words of three or four letters, when her husband found out about it. Douglass recalls: "[He] at once forbade Mrs. Auld to instruct me further, telling her, among other things, that it was unlawful, as well as unsafe, to teach a slave to read. . . . 'If you teach that nigger (speaking of myself) how to read, there would be no keeping him. It would forever unfit him to be a slave. He would at once become unmanageable, and of no value to his master. As to himself, it could do no good, but a great deal of harm. It would make him discontented and unhappy.' "[10]

For Douglass the experience "called into existence an entirely new train of thought." He now felt that he understood "the white man's power to enslave the black man," and although he was "conscious of the difficulty of learning [to read] without a teacher, [he] set out with high hope, and a fixed purpose, at whatever cost of trouble, to learn how to read."[11]

Notwithstanding the law, slaves did learn to read—taught by their masters, the slave master's children, white visitors to the plantation, and other outsiders, or other slaves.[12] But perhaps the most common avenue to literacy for the slaves was self-teaching, alone or in company with other illiterates. It was a slow, tedious process, for the only book generally available to them was the Bible, and the complexities it presented to beginner readers were not easily solved. But the slaves persisted, they learned, and after learning, adopted biblical language, proverbs, and themes for use in their everyday speech and in their improvised religious songs.

Not surprisingly, images of slaves teaching themselves or teaching other slaves to read are rarely encountered, though contemporaneous literary comment on the subject is considerable. As we have noted previously, many states had laws against providing schools for blacks, and, beginning in the 1830s, those of the Deep South were particularly stringent; the penalties imposed for whites included fines and even imprisonment and, for the slaves, floggings. In "The Chimney Corner" (fig. 27), Eastman Johnson explores the theme with great sensitivity, offering a sympathetic portrait of a fully grown man struggling to cope with the intricacies of the printed word. Although not technically a genre study, the image has narrative implications: the man (a slave) has

FIGURE 27. Eastman Johnson. "The Chimney Corner." 1863. Oil on cardboard. 15½ × 13¼ in. Munson-Williams-Proctor Institute, Museum of Art: Gift by exchange of Edmund B. Munson, Jr. Utica, New York.

found a private place to sit in his hovel, where he can concentrate on the task at hand; indeed, his concentration is so intense that he doesn't notice the fire has burned down to embers. There is no guarantee that he will be allowed to stay there as long as he wishes, but the viewer senses this to be an everyday activity for him, that he will return to the same spot on the next evening, find a comfortable position, open his book, and begin reading at the point where he left off the previous evening.

FIGURE 28. John Pettie and Dalziel. "Kalampin, the Negro." Pen and ink? Published in "Kalampin," by Countess de Gasparin. *Good Words* 4 (1863).

FIGURE 29. Arthur Burdett Frost. "A Negro Funeral in Virginia." Wood engraving. Published in *Harper's Weekly* 24 (1880).

FIGURE 30. William Ludlow Sheppard. "An Old-Time Midnight Slave Funeral."
Wood engraving by Schults. Published in *In the Brush . . .* , by Hamilton W. Pierson. New York: D. Appleton and Company, 1881.

FIGURE 31. George Fuller. "Negro Funeral." 1881. Oil on canvas. 17¾ × 30 in. Bequest of Anna Perkins Rogers. Courtesy of the Museum of Fine Arts, Boston (acc. no. 21.2174). Boston, Massachusetts.

FIGURE 32. George Fuller. "Negro Funeral. March 1858." Pencil on paper. Published in "Images of Slavery: George Fuller's Depictions of the Antebellum South," by Sarah Burns. *American Art Journal* 15 (Summer 1983). Photograph courtesy of Sarah Burns.

The theme is handled with equal warmth and sensitivity by an anonymous artist in "Kalampin, the Negro" (fig. 28), where a young girl and old man teach each other to read (see exx. of the handling of this theme in the postbellum era in figs. 127 and 128). A recurring motif in all the "reading" pictures shows the slaves, or ex-slaves, pointing to the words as they pronounce them, and this motif appears also in "preacher-reading-the-Bible" scenes.

The question arises whether these readers will ever become proficient enough to gain understanding of the text if they move at such a slow pace. That question did not overly trouble the slave, which is evident by the fact that hundreds of slave narratives were published in the nineteenth century by slaves who had learned to read by one or more of the methods discussed above. Their answers would have been that persistence will be rewarded.

FIGURE 33. John Antrobus. "A Plantation Burial." c. 1860. Oil on canvas. 53 × 81½ in. The Historic New Orleans Collection (acc. no. 1960.46). New Orleans, Louisiana.

FIGURE 34. "A Negro Funeral." Wood engraving. Published in "Rice Lands of the South," by T. Addison Richards. *Harper's New Monthly Magazine* 19 (1859).

Notes

1. Southern, *Music,* 38–39.

2. See further regarding the emergence of the black church in Southern, *Music,* 37–42, 71–80.

3. Svin'in, 20. *Picturesque Voyage.* The book was written in Svin'in's native Russian. According to Gleason in "Pavel Svin'in," 19, after the portfolio's publication it was lost from view for more than a hundred years. In 1930, Avrahm Yarmolinsky, editor, translated it into English and published it under the title *Picturesque United States of America, 1811, 1812, 1813, Being a Memoir on Paul Svinin, Russian Diplomatic Officer, Artist, and Author, Containing Copious Excerpts from his Account of His Travels in America. . . .* (New York: W. E. Rudge, 1930).

4. Svin'in, *Picturesque Voyage,* 20.

5. Bremer, *Homes,* 2:157–60.

6. Ibid.

7. See further in Jones, *Religious Instruction.* A Presbyterian minister, Jones was for many years Missionary of the Association for the Religious Instruction of Negroes in Georgia.

8. Long, *Pictures,* 19–20.

9. Pierson, *In the Brush,* 284–87.

10. Douglass, *Narrative,* 47.

11. Ibid.

12. See further about the prohibition of teaching slaves to read in John Belton O'Neall, *The Negro Law of South Carolina. . . . Collected and Digested by J. B. O.* (Columbia, South Carolina: Printed by John G. Bowman, 1848).

FIGURE 37. John William Orr. "Negro Quarters." Wood engraving. Published in "Sugar and the Sugar Region of Louisiana," by Thomas Bangs Thorpe. *Harper's New Monthly Magazine* 7 (1853).

formal and informal dances; dancing with musical accompaniment and dancing without music. Since dancing was a favorite pastime of black folk, it was not unusual for travelers in the South to come across a dance in progress, especially on Saturday nights, and almost always during the Christmas holidays, the one time of the year when most slaveholders gave their slaves respite from work for a period lasting from two or three days to as much as a week. Another time of the year when the masters were inclined to give slaves time off, if only for a night, was the harvest season, which slaves celebrated with "laying-bycrop jubilees," particularly in association with husking corn, which the slaves called "corn shuckings."

Of the sixteen illustrations in our collection of antebellum dance scenes (figs. 35–45 and 48–52), five depict group dances and the remainder focus on the dancing of couples or individuals. The artists are painstaking in their employment of details that would certify they had witnessed with their own eyes the events they depict and were making available to the public visual records of the everyday life of slaves. At the same time, the artists show concern for including enough exotica, enough "differentness," to entice the public to purchase their art works and to enable them to secure commissions from patrons, individual and institutional.

Informal Dancing of Couples

In the informal dance scenes, the focus generally is on one dancing couple, composed of a man and a woman, who are surrounded by onlookers and the musicians who provide music for the dancing. From one scene to the next, the artistic conventions observed by the artist hardly vary in nature: typically, the dancing couple is placed in the center or near center of the foreground; the musicians, seated on the ground or on barrels or boxes, are placed to the right or left of the dancers; the spectators consist of persons of all ages; and in some instances, whites watch from a distance in the background or middle ground. The spectators are not uniformly attentive, but those who do pay close attention actively participate in the performance—singing, clapping their hands, stomping on the ground, and responding to unusual capers with outbursts of encouragement. Conspicuously missing from the scenes are dancing couples consisting of adolescent boys and girls together, whereas couples composed of two boys or two young men are common.

The dance motifs used by artists in these antebellum pictures are largely similar to the motifs they used in depicting slave dancing in the colonial period, which we discussed earlier (see pp. 26–28). The men execute huge leaping steps, assume extravagant body positions and contortions of the limbs, constantly cross the legs, take heel-toe spins, and sometimes flourish a hat in the air. The women take daintier steps (though not always), lifting the ends of their skirts in curtsy fashion. In the solo dance scenes, the male is even more wildly energetic and freer with his arm movements, thrusting them back with dangling wrists or outstretching them to the side with palms turned downward, and often waving a hat as though it is an essential prop for the dance.

How the slaves typically spent their Sunday afternoons, particularly on plantations where there was no religious activity, is shown in "Negro Village on a Southern Plantation" (fig. 39) and "The Sabbath among Slaves" (fig. 40).

In the first of these pictures, two young men display their terpsichorean talents before a small but appreciative audience, accompanied by a fiddler, who also appears to be enjoying the performance. Assisting him with the dance music is a male who beats on a barrel temporarily transformed into a drum, and one of the dancers, who plays the bones.

The other picture (fig. 40) was published as an illustration in the autobiography of ex-slave Henry Bibb, its purpose to emphasize Bibb's complaint that slaves were not given moral instruction, had no one to read the Bible to them, and no one to preach the gospel: "Hence they resort to some kind of amusement. Those who make no profession of religion, resort to the woods in large numbers on that day to gamble, fight, get drunk, and break the Sabbath. This is often encouraged by slaveholders. When they wish to have a little sport of that kind, they go among the slaves and give them whiskey, to see them dance, 'pat Juber,' sing and play on the banjo."[1]

In sketching a scene the artist of course is able to catch only one moment of the action in his drawing, in the same way as for the photographer who snaps a picture. To understand what was going on before "the moment," or what will take place after "the moment," it can be useful to turn to written accounts, if available, that purport to describe the scene, or a similar one. In "Recollections of Southern Plantation Life," South Carolina planter Henry William Ravenel recalls the popularity of the jig during his youth in the 1830s–40s:

> The jig was an African dance and a famous one in old times, before more refined notions began to prevail. . . . It was strictly a dance for two, one man and one woman, on the floor at a time. It was opened by a gentleman leading out the lady of his choice and presenting her to the musicians. She always carried a handkerchief held at arm's length over her head, which was waved in a graceful motion to and fro as she moved. The step, if it may be so called, was simply a slow shuffling gait in front of the fiddler, edging along by some unseen exertion of the feet, from one side to the other—sometimes curtsying down and remaining in that posture while the edging motion from one side to the other continued.
>
> Whilst this was going on, the man danced behind her, shuffling his arms and legs in artistic style, and his whole soul and body thrown into the dance. The feet moved about in most grotesque manner stamping, slamming, and banging the floor not unlike the pattering of hail on the housetop. . . . Whenever any striking attitude was assumed, or unusual antics performed, there would be shouts of applause from the spectators.[2]

Beginning in the late 1840s, use of the word "jig" to apply generally to black dances gradually disappears in both written and pictorial sources, and it is replaced by more specific terms for characteristic plantation dances, such as those pictured in "The Breakdown" (fig. 44) and "Virginia Hoe-Down" (fig. 45). Some contemporary journalists linked the folk dances with geographical places, applying such names as the Virginny Breakdown, Alabama Kickup, Tennessee Double-shuffle, and Louisiana Toe-and-Heel, but there is no documentation for assuming that a slave dance originated in one state rather than another.[3] These dances were to be found all over the South. What we do note is that there was a tradition for dancers to imitate local birds and animals, such as in the dances called the Buzzard Lope, the Georgia Rattle-Snake, the Pigeon Wing, and others with similar names.

Informal Group Dances

Three pictures show slaves participating in group dancing outdoors on the plantation, as distinguished from watching others dance—"Evening at the Quarters" (fig. 35), "Old Plantation Play-Song" (fig. 41), and "The Festival" (fig. 48). In "Evening at the Quarters," the night is tranquil; the slaves are relaxing in various ways at the end of the day's work, some chatting with friends, others lolling around. The viewer's eyes are caught by a group moving in the middle ground left center of the picture, a group of mostly women. Joined by two men, they hold hands as they gaily skip around in circular formation, accompanied by a banjoist seated on a nearby porch to the left of the dancers. This ring dance, also called the "ring shout," was one of the most persistent survivals of an African tradition in the United States.

Though the "play-song" and the "festival" scenes involve many participants, in both instances the artists have focused attention on one or two couples in the center foreground of the pictures, whose dancing essentially is the same as the dancing of the couples discussed above.

Special Occasions

Christmas was a magical time for all members of the plantation community; few slaveholders dared deprive their workers of a vacation during the one time of the year when almost the entire South took holidays. The celebrating took the form of dancing, playing games, processions, and feasting, and often included entertaining the masters and their families who had come down to the Quarters to watch the fun, as in "The Holiday Dance" (fig. 42) and "Winter Holydays" (fig. 43). Above all, the Christmas season was a time for weddings.[4] It was not uncommon for the slaveholder, or a minister he had selected, to marry several couples at the same time in one group ceremony, and after the ceremony there was of course dancing and feasting.

Nathaniel Orr's "Christmas Eve Frolic" (fig. 49) and Lewis Miller's "Negro Dance" (fig. 50), which more than likely represent wedding festivities, are distinctive for the attire of the brides, who have on frilly white dresses with décolleté necklines and flowers in their hair, and of the grooms, who wear vests over their long-sleeved white shirts and white trousers. Adding a final touch to the elegance of the occasion are the white gloves worn by bride and groom. Both bridal pairs are excellent dancers, whose intricate movements are greatly appreciated by the admiring wedding guests.

Formal Balls

The present collection of antebellum dance scenes includes two portrayals of formal dances, the one, Christian Mayr's "Kitchen Ball at White Sulphur Springs" (fig. 51), a carefully conceived oil painting, and the other, Eyre Crowe's "A Negro Ball" (fig. 52), a pen-and-ink sketch, apparently hastily executed. Slave balls were not unusual, particularly in the Upper South; indeed, slave masters sometimes vied with each other in promoting elaborate balls for their charges, even to the extent of arranging for the use of appropriate rooms on the plantation, or renting hotel rooms in the cities, and providing refreshments. Both kinds of venues are represented in these pictures: a huge plantation kitchen in Virginia is converted into a temporary ballroom for Mayr's "Kitchen" ball (fig. 51), and a hotel ballroom has been rented in South Carolina for Crowe's "Negro" ball (fig. 52), which comes with crystal chandelier and potted plants placed about the room.

Eyre Crowe's pictorial report on the ball he visited in 1853 at Charleston, South Carolina, is hardly more than a cartoon, presenting more an impression than an actual representation of a crowded, probably noisy, ballroom with elaborately dressed people milling about and generally enjoying themselves. The artist makes no effort to particularize the dancers, though some of the dancing couples in the foreground of the picture do have traces of individuality. Clearly, music-making is the central activity of the scene: the five musicians who sit on a platform of sorts in the center background, high above the heads of the dancers, are having a very good time.

Like Crowe's picture, Christian Mayr's "Kitchen Ball" represents an actual event in 1838, but the dancers, unlike Crowe's, are real people who can be identified as belonging to the community. The English naval officer Frederick Marryat, who was touring in Virginia at the time Mayr was there, preserves in his journal, *Diary in America* (1839), a humorous anecdote about one of the musicians: "[Mayr] had painted a kitchen-dance in old Virginia, and in the picture he had introduced all the well-known colored people in the place; and the rest were the band of musicians, but I observed that one man was missing. 'Why did you not put him in,' inquired I. 'Why, Sir, I could not put him in; it was impossible; he never plays in tune. Why, if I put him in, Sir, he would spoil the harmony of my whole picture.' "[5]

Presenting a slice of the everyday life of ordinary people, Mayr's work is a textbook example of fine genre painting, which, in this instance, focuses on the theme of slave marriage. The pictorial conventions typically used by artists for such an event permit the picture to tell its own story: the wedding has taken place, and the scene shows the dance that comes afterward. Admiring eyes follow the bridal pair prancing on center stage, he in his white suit and she in her filmy white dress with décolleté neckline, flying ribbons, and orange-blossom headband. The members of the bridal party can easily be identified—the parents of the bride in the right foreground, a bridesmaid half-hidden in the background, other relatives in the left middle ground and background, and friends. Three in number, the dance musicians are seated along the right wall: the flutist, the violinist, and the cellist, who unfortunately is hidden to such extent by the mother of the bride that only his head and the lower part of his instrument can be seen.

Notwithstanding the formality of the occasions, a sense of joyful abandon seems to permeate the gathered company. While the predominance of string texture in the music for the dance in Virginia suggests that the party will be rather sedate, the energetic high-stepping and whirling of the dancers belie such an assumption. And the five-piece ensemble that is playing for the dance in Charleston (fig. 52), with its inclusion of tambourine and bones along with the two trumpets and cello, promises that affair to become quite lively as the night draws on. Clearly, all these dancers intend to have a great time.

Musical Forces for the Dancing

Typically, the musical forces for plantation dances consist of from two to four or five instruments. Judging by the evidence offered in the pictorial record, the fiddle is the backbone of the ensemble (figs. 39, 42, and 48–50); where there is a second instrument, most frequently it will be the banjo, either the flat-back instrument or the gourd-banjo. To this fiddle-banjo pair might be added a tambourine, the bones, and barrels used as drums and beaten with the hands, upturned stools used as drums and beaten with sticks, and the ground or floor used as a drum and beaten with sticks.

Despite the importance given the fiddle in antebellum artworks, which is indicated by its dominance of the dance ensemble—at least, on paper and canvas if not in the real world—artists were aware that the banjo, as an African instrument, had a favored place in plantation culture. Clergyman John Dixon Long, writing in the 1850s, pays tribute to the banjoist at the same time as he condemns the instrument: "The banjo is of all instruments the best adapted to the lowest class of slaves. It is the very symbol of their savage degradation. They talk to it, and a skillful performer can excite the most diverse passions among the dancers."[6]

If "pattin' Juba" is counted as an instrument, and that is how it functions in the context of plantation dances, it has a special place all its own in the musical ensemble. The patter may perform with the fiddle (fig. 42), with the banjo (figs. 40 and 44), with the banjo and fiddle (fig. 49), or with the full plantation ensemble of fiddle, banjo, and bones (figs. 43, 48, and 50). And, finally, the patter often serves as the only source of sounds for the dancing, though sometimes he may be accompanied by a singer, or may sing himself.

New Englander Lewis Paine, imprisoned in the South in 1841 for helping a slave to escape, gives explicit directions for performing the kind of pattin' he saw in Georgia: "Some one calls for a fiddle—but if one is not to be found, some one pats juber. This is done by placing one foot a little in advance of the other, raising the ball of the foot from the ground, and striking it in regular time, while, in connection, the hands are struck lightly together, and then upon the thighs. In this way they make the most curious noise, yet in such perfect order, it furnishes music to dance by."[7]

If the patter sings as he pats, it is not anything important, but rather "one of those unmeaning songs, composed rather for its adaptation to a certain tune or measure, than for the purpose of expressing any distinct idea."[8]

At the dance the musicians generally sit together (except for the patter), either to the left or right of the dancers but not within the circle of action. It is noteworthy that the patter is always placed near the dancing couple; indeed, in some instances, the patter might be taken for a third dancer, so clearly is he drawn into the arena of the central activity; see Bibb's "The Sabbath among Slaves" (fig. 40) and Felix Darley's "The Festival" (fig. 48). In several scenes, musicians sit in an elevated position above the heads of the gathered company—on top of a barrel, on a raised platform, or atop a huge pile of corn ears.

In one picture, "Old Plantation Play-Song" (fig. 41), there are no instruments, nor is there a patter, though three man-woman couples and two single males dance vigorously in the foreground and middle ground, and there are dancers among the shadowy figures in the background. It was not uncommon that dancers would choose to dance without musical accompaniment; many written records of the period include comment on the slaves' obsession with dancing, which was so great that they could, and would, proceed without the accompaniment of musical instruments.

The ensembles discussed above do not represent the only combinations of dance instruments used on the plantation. For a celebration in 1861, for example, the conventional three-piece instrumental forces are augmented by the addition of a large tambourine, which the performer holds high in the air as he beats it (fig. 49). And, predictably, the ensembles that play for "ballroom" dancing include a greater variety of instruments than do the ensembles for informal plantation dances. As discussed above, the cello plays with trumpets, tambourine, and bones in one ballroom group, and it joins the violin and flute in another ensemble. It may be, however, that the latter ensemble regularly included a fourth string player, if we are to accept the anecdote about Mayr, the artist, deliberately leaving the musician out of the scene when painting the "Kitchen Ball" picture (see p. 82).

Quite unusual is the band of six performers that plays music on a street in Tallahassee, Florida (fig. 36). Four are patters; they stand (with bent knees) in a square formation facing each other and pattin' zestfully. Two others are instrumentalists, who play with sticks on xylophone-like instruments that appear to be made of the jawbones (with the teeth left in) of a cow, horse, or ox. Generally, patters sit when performing, but pictures have survived that show them standing, bending from the waist and at the knees as they slap their thighs (figs. 40 and 48).

Finally, however, it was the three-piece plantation ensemble that came to typify the essential instrumentation of slave dance music, whether on or off the plantation, and that ensemble has been immortalized in William Sidney Mount's portraits of a fiddler, banjoist, and bones player (figs. 54–56).

Generally, the performance practice illustrated in these antebellum scenes is the kind customarily associated with American instrumental folk music: fiddlers hold the violin against the chest, except for the occasional fiddler who tucks his violin under his chin, as in "Winter Holydays" (fig. 43); bones players hold a pair of bones in each hand; banjoists rest their instrument against the thigh while playing. Banjoists play on a three-string or four-string banjo that invariably has an added "short fourth or fifth string."

Generally, tambourine players hold the instrument rather high in the air and give it a strong thump with the disengaged hand, as shown in Orr's "Christmas Eve Frolic" (fig. 49) and Crowe's "A Negro Ball" (fig. 52). But there is one intriguing image, George Heriot's "Minuet of the Canadians" (fig. 53), that shows a black player holding his tambourine shoulder-high in the right hand, extended out as far as it can go, and kicking the instrument with his left leg.[9] Although the scene shows a white ball in progress and, consequently, does not technically meet our rules for inclusion in the present collection of black genre pictures, the black tambourinist is presented here because of his unusual performance practice on the tambourine. Certainly, the image suggests how black musicians might have been handling the tambourine at the beginning of the nineteenth century in 1807.

Singing as They Worked

Antebellum images that show the slaves singing or otherwise making music as they work are rare. Presumably, their work consumed all their energy, with none left over for extraneous activity that did not contribute to lessening the workload, or, more probable, artists did not find that theme of sufficient interest to warrant transferring it to the sketchpad. One of the few extant illustrations is a George Fuller sketch (fig. 38), which depicts an overseer who has permitted his workers to take a brief rest from their labors, and they are spending the time in dancing to the fiddle music of one of their fellows.

The one plantation-work activity that did seem to intrigue artists was the corn-shucking festival, of which a number of images have survived. Since corn-husking scenes in general were perennial favorites with nineteenth-century artists, it was only natural that they should exploit the theme in their paintings of black folk. But there was a sharp difference between the "corn-husking bee" of white workers and the "corn shuckings" of the slaves, primarily because of the important role that music played in the activities of the latter.

"Husking Corn" (fig. 46) shows a fiddler sitting on top of a huge pile of corn ears, accompanying a group of six men singing with all their might as they husk the corn. In literary sources the black male voice generally is described in laudatory terms, such as "sonorous," "rich and melodious," "powerful and resonant." Presumably these corn huskers are producing sonorous sounds, probably in simple harmonies, and it is tempting to assume that the fiddler is improvising a melody above the harmonious sounds of the men. More common, however, was the slave-song performance practice whereby the carrier of

FIGURE 38. George Fuller. [Sketch for a Dance Scene.] Pencil on paper. Published in "Images of Slavery: George Fuller's Depictions of the Antebellum South," by Sarah Burns. *American Art Journal* 15 (Summer 1983). Photograph courtesy of Sarah Burns.

FIGURE 39. Christian Schussele (?). "Negro Village on a Southern Plantation." Wood engraving by William B. Gihon. *Aunt Phillis's Cabin, or Southern Life As It Is,* by Mary H. Eastman. Philadelphia: Lippincott, Grambo and Company, 1852.

FIGURE 40. Henry Bibb (?). "The Sabbath among Slaves." Wood engraving. Published in *Narrative of the Life and Adventures of Henry Bibb, an American Slave. Written by Himself.* New York: published by the Author, 1850.

FIGURE 41. James Henry Moser. "Old Plantation Play-Song, Putnam County, 1856." Wood engraving. Published in *Uncle Remus, His Songs and Sayings,* by Joel Chandler Harris. New York: D. Appleton and Company, 1893.

FIGURE 42. Henry Louis Stephens [pseud. for Charles Jacob Peterson]. "The Holiday Dance." Wood engraving by Bieler. Published in *The Cabin and the Parlor; Or, Slaves and Masters,* by J. Thornton Randolph, frontispiece. Philadelphia: T. B. Peterson, 1852.

FIGURE 43. "Winter Holydays in the Southern States. Plantation Frolic on Christmas Eve." Wood engraving. Published in "Christmas in the South," by Thomas Bangs Thorpe. *Frank Leslie's Illustrated Weekly Newspaper* 5 (1858).

FIGURE 44. "The Breakdown—American Home Scenes." Wood engraving. Published in *Harper's Weekly* 5/224 (1861).

FIGURE 45. Jacob A. Dallas. "Virginia Hoe-Down." Wood engraving. Published in "Remembrances of the Mississippi," by Thomas Bangs Thorpe. *Harper's New Monthly Magazine* 12 (1855).

FIGURE 46. "Husking Corn—American Home Scenes." Wood engraving. Published in *Harper's Weekly* 5/224 (1861).

the melody improvises on the tune and text to support the ever-changing verses, to which the chorus—here, the workers—respond with hearty refrains in a call-and-response mode.

To many spectators, the planter Daniel R. Hundley among them, the workers' songs were "usually wild and indescribable . . . mere snatches of song rather than any long continuous effort, but with an often recurring chorus, in which all join with a depth and clearness of lungs truly wonderful."[10] Artist Felix Darley uses a diptych format for his visual representation of a corn-shucking festival, "Sing, Darkeys, Sing" (fig. 47) and "The Festival" (fig. 48),

FIGURE 47. Felix Octavius Carr Darley. "Chorus—Sing, Darkeys, Sing." Wood engraving by Elias J. Whitney and Phineas F. Annin. Published in *"Uncle Tom's Cabin" Contrasted with Buckingham Hall, the Planter's Home . . .* , by Robert Criswell. New York: D. Fanshaw, 1852.

FIGURE 48. Felix Octavius Carr Darley. "The Festival." Wood engraving by Elias J. Whitney and Phineas F. Annin. Published in *"Uncle Tom's Cabin" Contrasted with Buckingham Hall, the Planter's Home . . .* , by Robert Criswell. New York: D. Fanshaw, 1852.

FIGURE 49. Nathaniel Orr. "Christmas Eve Frolic." Wood engraving. Published in *Maum Guinea and Her Plantation Children,* by Metta V. Victor, frontispiece. New York: Beadle and Company, 1861.

FIGURE 50. Lewis Miller. "Lynchburg—Negro Dance, August 18th, 1853." Abby Aldrich Rockefeller Folk Art Center (acc. no. 78.301.1, 17B). Williamsburg, Virginia.

FIGURE 51. Christian Mayr. "Kitchen Ball at White Sulphur Springs." 1838. Oil on canvas. 24 × 29½ in. North Carolina Museum of Art. Purchased with funds from the State of North Carolina. Raleigh, North Carolina.

first showing the slaves at work husking the corn, then showing them celebrating with a party after the work has been completed. In both scenes, white slave masters watch from positions in the middle ground or background. "Sing, Darkeys, Sing" (fig. 47) depicts a song leader sitting atop the pile of corn ears vigorously conducting the singing of the corn huskers seated at the bottom of the pile, who include men, women, and children. Though not all are totally involved in their tasks or in the singing, the widely opened mouths of those who are singing suggest that they are producing sounds of considerable volume, to which is added the noises of a male who beats with corn husks on a drum devised from an upturned, three-legged stool. (See pp. 182–89 for a discussion of postbellum corn-shuckings.)

The second scene of Darley's diptych, "The Festival" (fig. 48), depicts a typical slave dance: attention is focused on the musicians and a dancing couple in

FIGURE 52. Eyre Crowe. "A Negro Ball, Charleston, Ca. [*sic*], March 8, 1853." Pen and ink. Published in *With Thackeray in America,* by Eyre Crowe. New York: Charles Scribner's Sons, 1893.

FIGURE 53. George Heriot. "Minuet of the Canadians." 1807. Aquatint by J. C. Stadler. Reproduced in *Travels through the Canadas,* by George Heriot. London: R. Phillips, 1807.

FIGURE 54. William Sidney Mount. "Right and Left." 1850. Oil on canvas. 30 × 25 in. The Museums at Stony Brook, New York. Museum Purchase, 1956.

FIGURE 55. William Sidney Mount. "The Banjo Player." 1856. Oil on canvas. 36 × 29 in. The Museums at Stony Brook, New York. Gift of Mr. and Mrs. Ward Melville, 1955.

the foreground, while in the shadowy middle ground workers are eating, dancing, and playing games. The song leader of the corn-shucking event has now become the patter and the director of the dancers, whose fancy stepping holds spellbound at least two of the spectators. The patter shares the spotlight with the dancing couple and, at the same time, seems to have under control the musical forces, which consist of fiddle, banjo, and bones, in addition to his pattin'.

Meditative Music

Although valued primarily as dance instruments by antebellum artists, the fiddle and the banjo contributed also to the spirituality of slave life. The historical record is replete with accounts of how the slaves found relief from their oppression and despondency by making music. "The [improvised] songs of the slave," wrote the ex-slave and race-activist Frederick Douglass in 1845,

FIGURE 56. William Sidney Mount. "The Bone Player." 1856. Oil on canvas. 36⅛ × 29⅛ in. Bequest of Martha C. Karolik for the Karolik Collection of American Paintings, 1815–1865. Courtesy, Museum of Fine Arts, Boston (acc. no. 48.461). Boston, Massachusetts.

"represent the sorrows, rather than the joys, of his heart; and he is relieved by them, only as an aching heart is relieved by its tears."[11]

Among slaves who sought respite from their suffering and peace for their souls in playing instrumental music, one of the most articulate was violinist Solomon Northup. Born a free man, he was captured into slavery at the age of thirty-three, not to be rescued for twelve years, and the harrowing experience is recounted in his autobiography, published in 1853. "Alas," he wrote, "had it not been for my beloved violin, I scarcely can conceive how I could have endured the long years of bondage. . . . It was my companion—the friend of my bosom—triumphing loudly when I was joyful, and uttering its soft, melodious consolations when I was sad. Often, at midnight, when sleep had fled affrighted from the cabin, and my soul was disturbed and troubled with the contemplation of my fate, it would sing me a song of peace. On holy Sabbath days, when an hour or two of leisure was allowed, it would accompany me to some quiet place on the bayou bank, and, lifting up its voice, discourse kindly and pleasantly indeed."[12]

Six of our antebellum artworks present scenes that explore the theme of meditative instrumental music. First, there are the banjoist in "A Carolina Rice Planter" (fig. 57) and the young flutist in Eastman Johnson's "Negro Boy" (fig. 58).[13] Both obviously play for their own enjoyment and self-gratification. A third musician, depicted in George Fuller's "The Banjo Player" (fig. 59), presumably is entertaining his mother, but since she gives her full attention to the meal she is preparing, the young banjo player essentially is left alone in the musical web he has woven around them. Three other pictures show domestic scenes that center on instrumentalists playing for the enjoyment of their families during their leisure hours (figs. 60–62).

FIGURE 57. "A Carolina Rice Planter." Wood engraving. Published in "The Rice Lands of the South," by T. Addison Richards. *Harper's New Monthly Magazine* 19 (1859).

FIGURE 58. Eastman Johnson. "Negro Boy." c.1860. Oil on canvas. 14 × 17⅛ in. National Academy of Design. New York, New York.

FIGURE 59. George Fuller. "The Banjo Player." 1876. Oil on canvas. 17 × 21 in. [Location unknown]. Photograph courtesy of Sarah Burns.

Totally absorbed in their music-making, the young men in figures 57–59 stare into space, neither seeing nor hearing anything except the mellifluent sounds that they draw from their instruments. The "Rice Farmer" in all probability is enjoying a vacation day—he does not wear work clothes—freed not only temporarily from labor but also from the necessity of having to communicate with anyone or anything except his beloved banjo. Neither will anyone disturb the reverie of the young flutist, who plays on a homemade instrument, probably one he made himself, while sitting on the stoop of his slave cabin. The other banjoist has found a quiet place for his musical meditation in the kitchen, where the clutter of cooking utensils and furnishings do not prevent his escaping through music into his own private world.

An experience of artist George Fuller allows the viewer to peek behind the curtain, so to speak, of "The Banjo Player." During a visit to Montgomery, Alabama, in December 1857, Fuller hired a young banjoist to model for him, and later wrote to his sister: "The other day we had a real plantation Negro Banjo player—as a study for a full length—He played and sang most of the time (six hours) of his sitting, but would get sleepy at times.—We paid him two dollars for robbing him of so much of his Christmas jollity . . . the fellow really did make some harmony, and there was no want of zeal."[14]

John Ehninger's painting "Old Kentucky Home" (fig. 60) depicts a fiddler playing for the enjoyment of members of his immediate family, who have been joined by a young visitor from the Big House. We may assume that the fiddler carries the melody of the piece on his fiddle, while his son provides an accompaniment (chordal?) on the banjo. This is serious music, inappropriate for dancing or for accompanying nonsensical ditties. Although the father smiles slightly, no one else does; rather, the music has sent the mother into a pensive mood.

Eastman Johnson's "Life in the South" (fig. 61), also known as "Negro Life in the South" and in later years as "Old Kentucky Home," also shows a family, this time an extended one, assembled in the backyard of a dilapidated house, where they share a time of leisure.[15] The central figure, a man playing the banjo, is caught up in a private world of his own and is oblivious to the individuals about him. Standing to the left of the banjoist, a young boy gazes at him in wonderment; he is the only one who listens to the music, which serves primarily to furnish a background of sound for the varied activities going on. Perhaps the mother teaching her small son to dance in the foreground of the picture is conscious of the music's rhythms, but neither she nor the boy glances in the direction of the banjoist. The artist painted the work from life in 1859 at Washington, D.C., and it is probable that the models were slaves.

In another painting, "Confidence and Admiration" (fig. 62), Johnson has removed the banjoist and his young worshiper from the family scene to give them a canvas of their own. This is one of two paintings that Johnson

FIGURE 60. John Whetten Ehninger. "Old Kentucky Home." 1863. Oil on canvas. 15¼ × 9 in. Shelburne Museum. Shelburne, Vermont. Photograph by Ken Burris.

FIGURE 61. Eastman Johnson. "Life in the South" (also known as "Negro Life in the South" and in later years as "Old Kentucky Home"). 1859. Oil on canvas. 36 × 45¼ in. © Collection of the New-York Historical Society. New York, New York.

FIGURE 62. Eastman Johnson. "Confidence and Admiration," Study for "Negro Life in the South." 1859. Oil on canvas. Mead Art Museum. Amherst College (acc. no. 1958.48). Museum purchase. Amherst, Massachusetts.

produced "after parts of" images shown in "Negro Life in the South."[16] With searching detail the artist evokes the various emotions reflected in the man's face and captures the boy's expression of longing for the time when he will be able to play beautiful music like the banjoist (his father?).

Telling Folk Tales on the Plantation

A few sources before the Civil War refer to the slaves telling folk tales among themselves and to children of local planters. In 1851, Joseph Beckham Cobb writes, for example, that the slave repertory of tales included animal fables as well as stories about Jack-o'-the-lantern, the whippoorwill, and swamp oils.[17] Some of the earliest transcriptions of black folk tales also begin to appear in the American press around this time, including a black version of the creation myth published in the *Zion's Herald and Wesleyan Journal* (October 21, 1857) and a prototype of a Master-John tale, entitled "The Slave That Sold His Master," printed by the *Liberator* on March 16, 1860.

Antebellum artists apparently did not find scenes of slave story-telling as compelling or exotic a subject for depiction, however, as the singing and dancing of slaves. The illustrator Felix Darley supplies the single antebellum image in our collection of this genre, "Wild Bill, Walter and Utopia" (fig. 63). This scene depicts a black man, possibly a slave, and a young white couple who seem captivated by his fanciful story.

Sold Off to Georgy

Scenes of heavily chained coffle gangs trudging through the countryside from one slave market to the next—such as represented in "The Coffle Gang" (fig. 64) and "How Slavery Honors Our Country's Flag" (fig. 65)—goaded by slave traders with whips in hand, remind the viewer that the horrors of slavery are unceasing for the black folk caught in its grasp. It is bizarre that the slave fiddlers are forced to produce music under such tragic circumstances, but justified by the traders as necessary in order to prevent melancholy from erupting among the slaves. The double-file columns of prisoners frequently are led by two slaves playing fiddles or banjos, or often the gangs sing their "own wild hymns of sweet and mournful melody:"

> *See these poor souls from Africa*
> *Transported to America:*
> *We are stolen and sold to Georgia, will you go along with me?*
> *We are stolen and sold to Georgia, go sound the jubilee*

WILD BILL, WALTER AND UTOPIA.

FIGURE 63. Felix Octavius Carr Darley. "Wild Bill, Walter, and Utopia." Wood engraving by Leslie. Published in *Life in the South: A Companion to Uncle Tom's Cabin*, by Calvin Henderson Wiley. Philadelphia: T. B. Peterson, 1852.

FIGURE 64. "The Coffle Gang." Wood engraving. Published in *The Suppressed Book about Slavery . . .* , by George Carleton. New York: Carleton, Publisher, 1864.

FIGURE 65. "How Slavery Honors Our Country's Flag." Wood engraving. Published in *The Narrative of Amos Dressler,* by Amos Dressler. New York: American Anti-Slavery Tract Society, 1836. Courtesy of Oberlin College Library Anti-Slavery Collection, Special Collections. Oberlin, Ohio. Photograph by Lydia Dull.

See wives and husbands sold apart
The children's screams!—it breaks my heart;
There's a better day a-coming, will you go along with me?
There's a better day a-coming, go sound the jubilee.

Gracious Lord! when shall it be,_
That we poor souls shall all be free?
Lord, break them Slavery powers—will you go along with me?
Lord, break them Slavery powers, go sound the jubilee.

Dear Lord! dear Lord! when Slavery'll cease,
Then we poor souls can have our peace;
There is a better day a-coming, will you go along with me?
There is a better day a-coming, go sound the jubilee.[18]

Leaving the Plantation

Away from the plantation, black folk, as freedmen or "hired-out" slaves, on the one hand found themselves with more liberty and more control of minor aspects of their lives, but on the other hand with less genuine freedom and little respect, if any at all, from the white citizenry. The artworks that relate to this aspect of our study show African-Americans interacting with whites on urban streets, on country roads, in the workplace, in public inns and taverns, and, after the beginning of the Civil War, in the army camps and on the battle-fields.

Peddlers on the Streets

In urban centers, the often outlandish clothing and strange but tuneful cries of street peddlers attracted the interest of tourists, local historians and other writers, as well as illustrators. Two cityscapes are presented here (figs. 66 and 67) to suggest the kind of environment in which the black street peddler worked; then follows a small collection of images of these people, along with examples of the kinds of cries they sing in trying to persuade others to purchase their wares or their services (figs. 68–75).

FIGURE 66. Baroness Hyde de Neuville. "Corner of Greenwich and Dey Streets." 1810. Watercolor. I. N. Phelps Stokes Collection, Miriam and Ira D. Wallach Division of Art, Prints and Photographs, New York Public Library, Astor, Lenox and Tilden Foundations. New York, New York.

FIGURE 67. John William Hill. "City Hall and Park Row." 1830. Watercolor. I. N. Phelps Stokes Collection (Stokes 1830 E-81), Miriam and Ira D. Wallach Division of Art, Prints and Photographs. New York Public Library, Astor, Lenox and Tilden Foundations. New York, New York.

FIGURE 68. "Black Tom, the Little Sweep Ho of New York." Wood engraving. Published in *Gleason's Pictorial Drawing-Room Companion* 2 (1852).

WHEN a little boy just arrived in town from the country, for the first time, wakes up in the morning, he hears a sound which surprises and puzzles him not a little. It is the shrill piercing voice of a child, singing at the utmost stretch of his powers, a strange, wild song, of which the wondering country boy cannot make out a single word; for the very good reason that it has no words, but is a succession of strange inarticulate shrieks, modulated into a sort of tune, always nearly the same, and always recognised as the song of the Chimney Sweep.

FIGURE 69. William Croome. "Chimney Sweep." Print. Published in *City Cries; Or, A Peep at Scenes in Town by an Observer,* 16. Philadelphia: George S. Appleton, 1850.

WHO has not heard the song of the Hominy-man? Who can tell what are its words? There is but one verse. It is gabbled over with great rapidity, and the words "Hominy! beautiful Hominy!" occur more than once; but the remaining words are all Greek to the greater part of his hearers.

The hominy-man is decidedly the most musical of all the criers, and attracts most attention.

FIGURE 70. William Croome. "Hominy Man." Print. Published in *City Cries . . . ,* 80. Philadelphia: George S. Appleton, 1850.

THE Pepper-pot woman is not quite so noisy now as she was some twenty years since, when her song might be heard at any hour of the evening, in almost any part of the city:—

"Pepper-pot!
All hot! all hot!
Makee back strong!
Makee live long!
Come buy my Pepper-pot!"

FIGURE 71.   William Croome. "Pepper-Pot Woman." Print. Published in *City Cries . . .*, 96. Philadelphia: George S. Appleton, 1850.

SEA BASS! FINE SEA-BASS!

THE striped Bass is one of the best articles for the table which our Atlantic fish-market supplies. It is found in all the fish-markets, and is carried about the streets in wheelbarrows by venerable negroes. Pompey, whose portrait appears in the engraving, retails a great many from his one-wheeled carriage; and he will tell you that his sea-bass are perfectly fresh and sweet.

FIGURE 72.   William Croome. "Sea-Bass Man." Print. Published in *City Cries . . .*, 72. Philadelphia: George S. Appleton, 1850.

"Y'ere's the White Whitey-Wash!
Brown White-Wash!
Yellow Whitey-Wash!
Green White-Wash!
Wash, Wash!
I'm about!"

THE white-wash man, with his pail and long-handled brush, has laid aside his horse and saw, or other implements of winter labour, and sallied forth in quest of some tidy housewife in want of his services, and if the spring be fairly opened, he need not go far, for who is there that does not at that season require his services?

FIGURE 73. William Croome. "White-Wash Man." Print. Published in *City Cries . . . ,* 28. Philadelphia: George S. Appleton, 1850.

OLD, inform, bent with toil, the splitter of wood, axe in hand, plods along the streets, crying out in a shrill voice, "*Split wood! Split wood!*" Sometimes he adds to this cry a verse of poetry in the style of the African Songsters, quite hard to be understood by common people. This verse ends with a loud shout, or rather scream, which generally attracts the attention of some house-maid, who knows there is plenty of kindling wood in the cellar which she cannot use for want of splitting. She hastens to the front door and calls in old Sambo, making him very happy with an order to split all the kindling wood in the cellar.

FIGURE 74. William Croome. "Split-Wood Man." Print. Published in *City Cries . . . ,* 88. Philadelphia: George S. Appleton, 1850.

FIGURE 75. Thomas Waterman Wood. "Moses, the Baltimore Ven-
dor." 1858. Oil on canvas. 24⅛ × 15 in. The Fine Arts Museums
of San Francisco. Mildred Anna Williams Collection, 1944.7. San
Francisco, California.

Street Entertainers

Another urban type represented in the pictorial record during the mid-century years is the black street entertainer, singer, dancer, or instrumentalist. Somewhat a professional, he cannot obtain a good livelihood from dancing or playing the banjo on the streets, but he earns enough to get along. An itinerant, he is ready to entertain in any public place, can be found in inns and taverns, in the countryside as well as on the streets of the towns, and at large public gatherings, such as depicted in James Clonney's "Militia Training" (fig. 77). He may travel alone, picking up an accompanist wherever he finds one, as in "Virginia Hoe-Down" (fig. 45), or he may take along his own accompanist, a patter as in "Dancing for Eels" (fig. 76). The dance motifs artists use in these scenes essentially are the same as those associated with plantation dancing. Here are the same complicated cross-over steps, the hat flourishes, the heel-toe spins, the characteristic position of the wrists and palms, and the accompaniment provided by a patter.

FIGURE 76. James Brown. " 'Dancing for Eels'—A Scene from the New Play of *New-York As It Is,* as Played at the Chatham Theatre, New York." 1848. Lithograph by Eliphalet M. Brown and James Brown. Courtesy of the Library of Congress. Washington, D.C.

FIGURE 77. James Goodwyn Clonney. "Militia Training." 1841. Oil on canvas. 28 × 40 in. Courtesy of the Pennsylvania Academy of the Fine Arts. Bequest of Henry C. Carey (The Carey Collection). Philadelphia, Pennsylvania.

The dancers who entertain Clonney's militiamen and their gathered company are a sophisticated pair, see "Sketches of Dancing Man and Other Studies" (fig. 78), "Negro Boy Dancing" (fig. 79), and "Negro Boy Singing and Dancing" (fig. 80). Although a white fiddler plays for the dancing in this scene, the presence of the black fiddler suggests that he, not the white fiddler, is the regular accompanist. Integration was practically nonexistent in the 1840s, particularly among travelers on the road. Evidence of Clonney's meticulous concern for authentic representation and detail is revealed in the sketches and studies he made of the dancers who are featured in his oil painting (figs. 78–80), and in the two studies for "A Dance on a Stone Boat" (figs. 81 and 82). The stone boat,

FIGURE 78. James Goodwyn Clonney. "Sketches of Dancing Man and Other Studies." [1841]. Graphite on buff paper. 9⅜ × 11⅝ in. Gift of Maxim Karolik for the Karolik Collection of Watercolors and Drawings. Courtesy, Museum of Fine Arts, Boston (acc. no. 60.1007). Boston, Massachusetts.

FIGURE 79. James Goodwyn Clonney. "Negro Boy Dancing." 1839. Wash. 8¼ × 6⅛ in. Study for "Militia Training." M. and M. Karolik Collection. Courtesy, Museum of Fine Arts, Boston (acc. no. 62.215). Boston, Massachusetts.

FIGURE 80. James Goodwyn Clonney. "Negro Boy Singing and Dancing." 1839. Black ink with highlight scraping on beige paper. 7⅝ × 5½ in. Study for "Militia Training." M. and M. Karolik Collection. Courtesy, Museum of Fine Arts, Boston (acc. no. 62.216). Boston, Massachusetts.

FIGURE 81. James Goodwyn Clonney. Study for the Central Figure from "A Dance on a Stone Boat." [date unknown] Graphite on buff paper. 12¾ × 8¾ in. Gift of Maxim Karolik for the Karolik Collection of Watercolors and Drawings. Courtesy, Museum of Fine Arts, Boston (acc. no. 60.994). Boston, Massachusetts.

FIGURE 82. James Goodwyn Clonney. Study for "Dance on a Stone Boat (small composition)" [184?]. Graphite on brown paper. Gift of Maxim Karolik for the Karolik Collection of Watercolors and Drawings. Courtesy, Museum of Fine Arts, Boston (acc. no. 55.712). Boston, Massachusetts.

which serves as a dancing platform for the central figure, is simply a sledge used for hauling stone from one place to another. The dancer in the foreground center has struck just the correct pose of the typical plantation dancer, and he receives enthusiastic support from the patter on the extreme right of the picture.

Contraband and Freedmen

The beginning of the Civil War in 1861 almost immediately brought about new relations between the nation's nearly four million slaves and their masters. Thousands of slaves ran away from the plantations seeking protection behind the lines of the Union forces. Large numbers were forced to work behind the army lines in the Confederacy, and tens of thousands simply fled, seeking freedom wherever they could find it.

The federal government, having no consistent policy regarding the runaways, permitted army officers to handle matters as they pleased, with the result that in some places fugitive slaves were welcomed by the Union Army, and in other places they were rejected. In the spring of 1861, Brigadier General Benjamin F. Butler made a decision that would nudge the federal government into action when he declared that the slaves who escaped into Union camps that were under his jurisdiction would be treated as "contraband of war," and consequently would not be returned to their masters. Finally, in August of that year, Congress passed a Confiscation Act that legally recognized fugitive slaves as "contraband of war"—that is, "property"—to be freed by Union forces when captured. During the course of the war, the journalists and artist-reporters who followed the troops behind the lines sent thousands of articles and sketches back to their magazines and newspapers, which quickly transformed the latter into engravings to be published in the press. Some artists later used their sketches as the bases for oil paintings that were exhibited in prestigious art shows, hung in museums, and made available to the public as prints.

In response to the public's ever-increasing interest in the black man, combat artists scoured the plantations and military encampments in search of the strange, the exotic, and the sensational in portraying images of the slaves. In the process they developed new themes. A number of paintings and drawings have survived, for example, that depict fugitive slaves fleeing the plantations on foot and on horseback, through swamps, open fields, and wooded areas.

Another popular subject was the black serviceman: black soldiers are shown in battle scenes, or standing stiffly at attention in platoon formation, or enjoying recreation breaks. Finally, there are artworks that show the daily aspects of military-camp life for the slave refugees. Since most of the pictorial journalists were coming into contact with slavery for the first time, the everyday activities of the slaves proved to be as intriguing subjects for pictorial recording as did the images of slaves in flight from the hated plantations or black servicemen in action.

Highly skilled, Civil War artist-journalists could make quick sketches on the spot with a few decisive strokes, which later would be developed into finished drawings, the artists filling in details according to their memory of the scene or to the penciled notes they had jotted down on their sketch pads. Under some circumstances, an artist might have to re-create a scene with only the detailed report of an eyewitness to guide him. By the time of the Civil War years, the cameraman had begun to take on the function of on-the-spot reporting, and his photographs were used in the same way as the sketches were used to serve as a basis for the finished artwork.

Our collection includes ten images that portray particulars of the cultural world in which the slave lived during the period of his transition from enslavement to emancipation (figs. 83–92). The Emancipation Proclamation of 1863 of course liberated only slaves in states that had seceded from the Union, and it was not until 1865, with the passage of the Thirteenth Amendment, that all the slaves in the nation finally were freed. In the social confusion of the time, slaves found themselves in one or more of several roles: while the large majority remained on the plantations until informed of their emancipation by the slaveholders or Northern officers, sizable numbers obtained freedom by running away from the plantation. A third group falls into the class of contraband, who generally came under the supervision of the Union forces or the American Freedmen's Aid Association; a fourth group of indeterminate numbers lived more or less independently as refugees; and, finally, thousands of men chose to join the armed forces, as servicemen or laborers, on the Confederate side (figs. 88 and 91) as well as the Union.

Edwin Forbes's carefully drawn "The War in Virginia" (fig. 83) presents a detailed pictorial description of an extended family of contrabands, who, loaded down with all their possessions, slowly make their way down the road to the safety of a federal camp. Three generations are represented—the women, children, and an old man ride in a battered old wagon; the younger men walk, except for a lone horse rider—but there is no suggestion of the sounds of camaraderie normally associated with movement of so large a black group. The subdued exchange among two or three of the wagon riders serves only to intensify the depressing tone of the scene; one can almost hear the sound of animal hoofbeats piercing the thick silence. Clearly this is a time of great apprehension for the contrabands.

The editor of *Frank Leslie's Illustrated Famous Leaders and Battle Scenes of the Civil War,* the source in which this artwork was published, was so moved that he felt the need to add his own commentary to the obvious message given out by the picture.

> The negro furnishes, in his various phases of existence, wonderful studies for the artist and philosopher. Never, perhaps, has a race seen such a moment as during the Civil War, when the chains of bondage were breaking from the limbs of 4,000,000 of men. The distant roar of battle was to them a sound of deliverance. With all the uncouth, odd and queer manifestations of joy they prepared to reach the camp of the delivering Yanks. Yoking together most incongruous teams before the farm wagons of their fled masters, with ass and ox and horse, with household gear queerly assorted, with useless truck and little that could rarely serve them, they started for the Promised Land, and might often have been seen coming in as our artist, a most close friend of nature, depicted them, with his usual felicity of portraiture.[19]

FIGURE 83. Edwin Forbes. "The War in Virginia—Contrabands Coming into the Federal Camp." Wood engraving. Published in *Frank Leslie's Illustrated Famous Leaders and Battle Scenes of the Civil War*, edited by Louis Shepheard Moat. New York: Mrs. Frank Leslie, 1896.

Forbes's drawing is a perfect metaphor for the movement of black folk from slavery to liberation, the dark, threatening skies suggesting how stormy the future may be. At the same time, the picture presents a secondary theme—the importance of music to the slaves—which can be read as counterbalancing to some extent the general gloom and fear of the primary image.

Carrier of the secondary theme is the young man who leads the unkempt group, holding a fiddle under his arm. Given his own space at the far right of the picture, he does not have to compete, as do the picture's other objects, with the people, animals, wagon, weeds growing by the wayside, and so on. He moves into the light away from the dark that envelopes most of the scene, his fiddle extending before him by a foot or so. He is the leader, the future. His people carry with them the basic things they need to begin a new life, of necessity having left behind all but their essential belongings, of which the most important is their music, here represented by the fiddle motif. The fiddle represents also their continuity with the past: the song that has sustained them for almost 250 years of slavery will be there to help them cope with the future.

Whether the creator of this scene intended the viewer to perceive the intent of the picture as suggested here is a matter of conjecture. Perhaps our artist was merely depicting the contrabands, "with his usual felicity of portraiture," as he saw them. Or, perhaps he was simply using the black-man-with-fiddle motif as a symbol of the black man's place in American society.

Freedom in the Camps

The Civil War genre pictures generally are set in military or contraband camps, where the fugitives and contraband engage in the same kinds of cultural activities as they did on the plantations. They take part in religious services (figs. 84 and 85), dance to amuse themselves (figs. 86 and 87), and entertain others with their dancing (figs. 88 and 90). The striking difference between the present and the past is that the contraband are free to worship as they please, freed of the white presence demanded by the laws of the southern states. And if they choose to dance for others, they expect payment for their services.

Two scenes that show worship services in progress differ sharply in style and content. In "The Contraband Camp at City Point—An Evening Prayer Meeting" (fig. 84), artist Joseph Becker has caught an open-air, nocturnal meeting of the contraband at a quiet moment in the service: the worshipers listen intently to the preacher, several with bowed heads, some with closed eyes, and a few with hands held in a prayer position. The relatively large number of individuals that are present include children and adults of all ages, and the reflection of the campfires and altar candles on their faces contributes to the somber mood that pervades the scene.

FIGURE 84. Joseph Becker. "The Contraband Camp at City Point—An Evening Prayer Meeting." Wood engraving. Published in *Frank Leslie's Illustrated Weekly Newspaper* 19 (1864).

William Sheppard's "Prayer Meeting in a Contraband Camp" (fig. 85), referring to the same theme, presents a wildly contrasting mood. His worshipers, crowded into a small, dark cabin, where the formal service has concluded, sing loudly, clap their hands, dance, and otherwise give evidence of spirit possession. It well may be that those who move about so energetically are executing the holy dance called the "the shout."

Several of the motifs appearing in Sheppard's picture later became identified with nineteenth-century pictorial representation of the religious emo-

FIGURE 85. William L. Sheppard. "Prayer Meeting in a Contraband Camp—Washington, 1862." Wood engraving. Published in *My Story of the War . . . ,* by Mary A. Livermore. Hartford, Connecticut: A. D. Worthington and Company, 1889.

tionalism of the black folk church, such as individuals on their knees loudly singing or/and praying, worshipers clapping their hands and stomping their feet, worshipers in dance postures, and individuals waving one hand in the air as they sing or shout. By the mid-century years, artists were beginning to link these motifs and similar ones with the theme of black religious dance.

The literature of the Civil War is replete with descriptions of slave worship practices, in particular the singing, which rarely failed to fascinate white listeners. An anonymous visitor in Hampton, Virginia, describing his experience among the contraband, remembers some of the verses of the song he heard:

> Last evening I took a stroll among the contrabands at their rendezvous. Some of them are in a most destitute condition, and they all live in constant terror of "something dat'll happen yet and carry us poor darkies all off." . . . I visited a large square house by the seashore, where some hundred of them were. I asked one of the negroes sitting by the door outside to sing for me. "I don't sing nothin' but Doctor Watson's [Watts's] invotional hymns," was the reply. I urged him to sing one of them, when he commenced in a low, murmuring, wailing, whining voice:

FIGURE 86. Francis H. Schell. "Yanks Expedition—Extempore Musical and Terpsichorean Entertainment at the U.S. Arsenal, Baton Rouge. Under the patronage of the 41st Mass., the 131st N.Y. and 25th Conn. Volunteers—Contraband Children." Wood engraving. Published in *Frank Leslie's Illustrated Weekly Newspaper* 15 (1863).

FIGURE 87. Theodore Russell Davis. "Camp of Negro Refugees." Wood engraving. Published in *Harper's Weekly* 9 (1865).

Jesus'll git us out o' dis,
Jesus'll git us out o' dis,
An' we'll go home to Can'an,
An' we'll go home to Can'an.

Heb'n 's a comin' by and bye,
Heb's 's a comin' by and bye,
An' we'll go home to Can'an,
An' we'll go home to Can'an. Etc.

As he sung [*sic*], some twenty or thirty blacks flocked around him, men and women, and joined him in the chorus. Their voices were clear and full of music, untutored indeed, but rich with a sincerety [*sic*] and feeling that was really impressive. The plaintive music grew louder and louder as voice after voice was added to its power, until the performance sounded like a choral service, to which the waves chaunted their vesper anthem in response.[20]

In scenes showing the contraband dancing for their own amusement—for example, Francis Schell's "Yanks Expedition" (fig. 86) and Theodore Russell Davis's "Camp of Negro Refugees" (fig. 87)—or dancing for the entertainment of white soldiers, as in Frank Vizetelley's "Night Amusements in the Confederate Camp" (fig. 88), Winslow Homer's "A Bivouac Fire on the Potomac" (fig. 90), and "View on the James River Canal" (fig. 91), artists draw freely upon motifs that by the 1860s had long been associated with the depiction of slave dancing. Dancers are shown with the body bent sharply forward or backward from the waist, the knees bent, arms outstretched to the side or back, palms of the hands turned down with fingers outstretched, and a great deal of heel-toe prancing. The best artists took meticulous care in trying to capture the essence of black dancing, striving to catch the exact pose, precise expression, and realistic nuances of body language.

Winslow Homer's central figure in "A Bivouac Fire on the Potomac" (fig. 90), provides the opportunity to study an artist's method in transcribing the movements of a black dancer to oil on canvas. Some art historians regard his preparatory study of the figure, given its own canvas in "Soldier Dancing" (fig. 89), as one of the most "celebrated" dancers in the history of American art.

FIGURE 88. Frank Vizetelley. "Night Amusements in the Confederate Camp." Wood engraving. Published in *Illustrated London News* 42 (1863).

FIGURE 89. Winslow Homer. "Soldier Dancing." Study for "A Bivouac Fire on the Potomac." Graphite on cream wave paper. 9$\frac{7}{16}$ × 6$\frac{1}{8}$ in. Cooper-Hewitt National Design Museum, Smithsonian Institution/Art Resource. Gift of Charles Saraget Homer (acc. no. 1912-12-134, verso). New York, New York.

FIGURE 90. Winslow Homer. "A Bivouac Fire on the Potomac." Wood engraving. Published in *Harper's Weekly* 5 (1861).

Predictably, the dance instruments that appear in these wartime scenes are those having a longtime affiliation with black dance. First and foremost is the fiddle, often accompanied by the banjo, and almost always accompanied by pattin' (fig. 91). At times, however, the banjo serves as the only dance instrument. We pointed out earlier that the contraband pictures differ little from plantation scenes except for the background settings, but there is one other, rather significant, distinction: the contraband pictures are filled with admirers of all ages who watch the dancing, from babies in their mothers' arms to the elderly. This is particularly noticeable in the camp scenes, which are crowded with white soldiers and officers, all of whom give close attention to the dancing as if they have not seen anything like it before, which they probably have not. They will carry accounts of the black man's culture back to their communities, and from their ranks will come the first collectors of slave songs, tales, and sermons.

The subject matter of one of the Civil War pictures, Winslow Homer's "Defiance: Inviting a Shot before Petersburg" (fig. 92), calls for special comment. Here the black banjoist is taken out of his usual stereotypical role of entertaining others with his banjo playing—in this case, the soldiers of the Union Army—to become a participant in the scheme to draw enemy fire and goad the enemy into attacking.

FIGURE 91. "View on the James River Canal, Near Balcony Falls—Rebel Troops Going from Lynchburg to Buchanan, on Their Way to Western Virginia." Wood engraving. Published in *Harper's Weekly* 5 (1861).

FIGURE 92. Winslow Homer. "Defiance: Inviting a Shot Before Petersburg, Virginia." 1864. Oil on panel board. 12 × 18 in. Detroit Institute of Arts (acc. no. 51.66). Founders Society purchase with funds from Dexter M. Ferry, Jr. Detroit, Michigan.

Notes

1. Bibb, *Narrative,* 23.
2. Ravenel, "Recollections," 768.
3. A listing of these dances appears in "Juba at Vauxhall," *Illustrated London News* (August 1848), 77.
4. See further in "An Englishman in South Carolina, December 1860 and July 1862," in *Continental Monthly* 3 (January–June 1863): 115–16. See also Genovese, *Roll, Jordan, Roll,* 475–80.
5. Marryat, *Diary,* 272.
6. Long, *Pictures,* 18.
7. Paine, *Six Years,* 89.
8. Northup, *Twelve Years,* 100.
9. Though this is not an African-American genre scene, we include it here because of the spectacular choreographic movements of the black tambourinist, which has implications for performance practice of black dance music to come, especially in the music called jazz.
10. Hundley, *Social Relations,* 345.
11. Douglass, *Narrative,* 101.
12. Northup, *Twelve Years,* 99.

13. "Negro Boy" won Johnson election to the National Academy of Design in 1860 as a full Academician.
14. Burns, "Images," 49.
15. Hills, *Eastman Johnson*, 32. It was "Negro Life in the South" that established Johnson's reputation as a major artist and earned him election to the National Academy of Design in 1859 as an Associate.
16. Ibid., 31. Johnson did other paintings "after parts of" his major work, "Negro Life in the South," which are, nevertheless, independent works. Another is "Southern Courtship."
17. Cobb, *Mississippi Sketches*, 98–99.
18. Brown, *Harp*, 29.
19. *Frank Leslie's Illustrated Famous Leaders*, 401.
20. "Religious Trust," 3.

PART III

THE
POSTBELLUM
ERA

The Black Preacher
as an Institution

After the Civil War, artists were compelled to construct new images of the black man and his culture that would conform with his changed position in the American social and political world. Our collection includes 168 works of art that represent the new social world of the emancipated African-American after the war (figs. 93–260). In terms of numbers, artists continued to focus on rural types in their postbellum scenes, this reflecting the fact that the ex-slaves largely remained on the plantations after Emancipation and continued to work in the fields—only now they were working for themselves and depending upon farming to become the source of their livelihood. Although fewer in number, urban types, too, attracted the attention of postbellum artists. Many of the freedmen who fled to urban areas of the North and the South after the war entered occupations formerly closed to them, where their activities stimulated some artists to depict the urban ex-slave developing a new lifestyle in a new environment.

Of all the subjects that commanded the attention of postbellum artists and writers, the most discussed was the religiosity of the freedman, particularly that of the black preacher. The priest-shaman in Africa become the preacher (or preacher-conjurer) on the plantations of the United States, his roots lay deep in the history of American slavery and, within the limits prescribed by his servitude, he flourished as both the spiritual and temporal leader of the black community. As a slave, he often commanded the respect of the planters, and sometimes he was given a measure of authority and responsibility so that he could minister to the religious needs of his fellow slaves or assist the white missionary in charge of religious education on the plantation.

121

After Emancipation it was the black preacher who exerted leadership in the movements of the freedmen and free blacks to secede from white churches and establish their own.

During the last quarter of the nineteenth century, the black church expanded rapidly (see previous discussion, p. 44). The oldest black denominations, particularly the African Methodist Episcopal and African Methodist Episcopal Zion Churches, saw membership increase enormously in their congregations, which had been established in the early nineteenth century, and they witnessed the founding of new congregations across the nation. In the South, new denominations came into being: black members of the white Primitive Baptist Church withdrew from the mother church in 1865 to form the Colored Primitive Baptist Church, and black Methodists left the white Methodist Episcopal Church (South) in 1870 to found the Colored Methodist Episcopal Church (in 1954 the name was changed to Christian Methodist Episcopal). Nevertheless, the white Methodist Episcopal Church (South) aggressively recruited ex-slave preachers to bring in converts, setting up organizing conferences for that purpose as early as 1867 and establishing thereafter new congregations for blacks within the jurisdiction of the white mother church.

Among the Baptists, whose autonomy gives them full control over their affairs, congregations banded together to form, first, state conventions and, then, national conventions: the National Baptist Convention in 1880, and the National Baptist Convention, Inc., in 1895. But the most striking development of the period was the emergence of Pentecostal churches in the 1890s, of which the Church of God in Christ became best known. The newly surfacing black denominations of the late nineteenth century would exert enormous influence on cultural development in the black community, particularly in the area of music.

More than one-third of the 168 pictures in our collection of postbellum artworks focus on the black preacher as a folk institution. He is depicted not only as a minister conducting formal and informal religious services, but also in his pastoral roles as counselor, mediator, comforter, consoler, healer, and friend. Artists represent him as self-assured, charismatic, even arrogant, and confident of his ability to be all things to his people. One source of his power and authority of course is his literacy, which gives him direct access to the Bible and qualifies him to assume leadership of his people.

Not that all black preachers could read, but, notwithstanding the state laws and city ordinances during slavery that had prohibited the teaching of blacks to read, whether free or enslaved, large numbers of black churchmen became literate. If a preacher could not read, he memorized the Bible to such an extent that his illiteracy often went undetected. Another source of his confidence was the fact that God had determined that he become a preacher. An anonymous man of God explained to the missionary W. L. Clarke in 1869:

Yer see I am a preacher. De Lord called me once when I was workin'. It would take long time to tell all he did, how I hole back and draw away, and how he pull me on and down on my knees, and all that; but I'll sense it to you quick. He call me and told me in imagination, you know, that he wanted me to preach. I told him I didn't know enough—that I was ig'nant, and the folks would laugh at me. But he drew me on and I prayed. I prayed out in the woods, and every time I tried to get up from my knees He would draw me down again. An' at last a great light came down sudden to me, a light as big as the moon, an' struck me hard on the head and on each shoulder and on the bress, here and here and here (striking himself). And den same time warm was in around my heart, and I felt de Book was there. An' my tongue was untied, and I preach every since and is not afraid. I can't read de Book, but I has it here, I has de text, and de meanin', and I speaks as well as I can, and de congregation takes what the Lord gives me.[1]

Postbellum images of the preacher portray him in a wide variety of activities: in the pulpit on a Sunday morning, arm uplifted and eyes blazing as he moves steadily toward the climactic point of his sermon (figs. 93–100, 102, 104–106); officiating at weddings (figs. 131 and 133), at baptismal ceremonies (figs. 137–139), and at funerals and burials (figs. 101 and 140). Along with his exhorters and church elders he is depicted as a leader of informal worship services held in the woods—camp meetings (fig. 117) and revival meetings (figs. 113–114)—and of prayer meetings held in praise cabins and the barnlike praise houses (figs. 105, 110, and 113–116). He leads the singing at religious services, clapping his hands and inciting the congregation to follow his lead (fig. 112). He counsels his members at informal gatherings (figs. 118–120), and he visits them in their homes (figs. 107–109). Above all, the preacher tends to the spiritual needs of his people, accepting their strange religious practices—labeled "heathenish" by both the black and the white church establishments—and encouraging their exotic expressive culture in song and dance (figs. 121–124).

Collectively, these images document the authority and power of the emancipated preacher in his own social world, peopled by ex-slaves and free African-Americans, who finally have been liberated from the immediate control of the white masters. "Three things characterized this religion of the slave," wrote sociologist W. E. B. Du Bois in 1901, "—the Preacher, the Music, and the Frenzy." According to Du Bois, "The Preacher is the most unique personality developed by the Negro on American soil. A leader, a politician, an orator, a "boss," an intriguer, an idealist,—all these he is, and ever, too, the centre of a group of men, now twenty, now a thousand in number."[2]

Most numerous of our "preacher pictures" are the portraits, real and fictive, depicting clergymen in various postures as they conduct formal or informal services in the church or other places of worship (figs. 93–106). In nine scenes

FIGURE 93. Charles Stanley Reinhart. "A Colored Preacher." 1889. Crayon. Published in *Harper's Weekly* 34 (1890).

FIGURE 94. Arthur Burdett Frost. "He P'int at Me." 1898. Mixed media. Published in "The Second Wooing of Salina Sue," by Ruth M. Stuart. *Harper's New Monthly Magazine* 98 (1898).

(where the artists have *not* included views of the congregations) three ministers are caught at climactic points in their sermons: Arthur Frost's figure "He P'int at Me" (fig. 94) shows the elderly preacher with right hand lifted in accusation of someone sitting before him; Edward Windsor Kemble's preacher in "He Preached a Powerful Sermon" (fig. 95) clasps his hands together as he summarizes his remarks; and an elderly man waving his clenched fist in the air is pictured in "He'd Call dem Scriptures Out" (fig. 102).

The elderly minister in Charles Reinhart's "A Colored Preacher" (fig. 93), in contrast, is shown reading from the Scriptures, totally absorbed in the matters at hand. And the novel format of a strip sequence of five scenes is used by photographer Leigh Richmond Miner to tell the story of "An Ante-bellum Sermon" (figs. 96–100), capturing the characteristic gestures and poses of the old-time black preacher.

FIGURE 95. Edward Windsor Kemble. "He Preached a Powerful Sermon, and at Its
Close Told Something of His Life." 1904. Pen and ink. Published in *The Heart of
Happy Hollow,* by Paul Laurence Dunbar. New York: Dodd, Mead and Company,
1904.

FIGURE 96. Leigh Richmond Miner. "An Ante-Bellum Sermon." Photograph. *Joggin' Erlong,* by Paul Laurence Dunbar, 74–78. New York: Dodd, Mead and Company, 1906.

FIGURE 97. Leigh Richmond Miner. "An Ante-Bellum Sermon." Photograph. *Joggin' Erlong.*

FIGURE 98. Leigh Richmond Miner. "An Ante-Bellum Sermon." Photograph. *Joggin' Erlong.*

FIGURE 99. Leigh Richmond Miner. "An Ante-Bellum Sermon." Photograph. *Joggin' Erlong.*

FIGURE 100. Leigh Richmond Miner. "An Ante-Bellum Sermon." Photograph. *Joggin' Erlong.*

FIGURE 101. Edward Windsor Kemble. [The Funeral Sermon.] Pen and ink. Published in *330 Drawings by Edward Windsor Kemble,* collected and arranged by Newton Chisneil. Brooklyn, New York: n.p., 1896.

FIGURE 102. Edward Windsor Kemble. "He'd Call dem Scriptures Out." Pen and ink. Published in *Plantation Songs and Other Verses*, by Ruth McEnery Stuart. New York: D. Appleton and Company, 1916.

FIGURE 103. J. W. Otto. "I Acknowledge I Did Wrong,/ I Stayed in de Wilderness Mos' Too Long—." Photograph. Published in *Plantation Songs for My Lady's Banjo . . .* , by Eli Shepperd. New York: R. H. Russell, 1901.

FIGURE 104. David Hunter Strother [pseud. Porte Crayon]. "The Negro Preacher [Charleston, South Carolina]." Wood engraving. Published in "On Negro Schools," by David Strother. *Harper's New Monthly Magazine* 49 (1874).

FIGURE 105. Alfred R. Waud. "Prayer-Meeting." Wood engraving. Published in "Scenes on a Cotton Plantation." *Harper's Weekly* 11 (1867).

FIGURE 106. J. Campbell Phillips. "The Gospel." 1899. Pen and ink. *Plantation Sketches* [artist's portfolio]. New York: R. H. Russell, 1899. Print Collection, Miriam and Ira D. Wallach Division of Art, Prints and Photographs. New York Public Library, Astor, Lenox and Tilden Foundations. New York, New York.

FIGURE 107. Edward Windsor Kemble. "Rev. Ezekiel Moses." Pen and ink. Published in "The Social Life of the Southern Negro," by W. T. Hewetson. *Chautauquan* 26 (1897).

FIGURE 108. Edward Windsor Kemble. "The Preacher." 1886. Pencil on paper. Published in "Mrs. Stowe's Uncle Tom at Home in Kentucky," by James Lane Allen. *Century Magazine* 34 (1887).

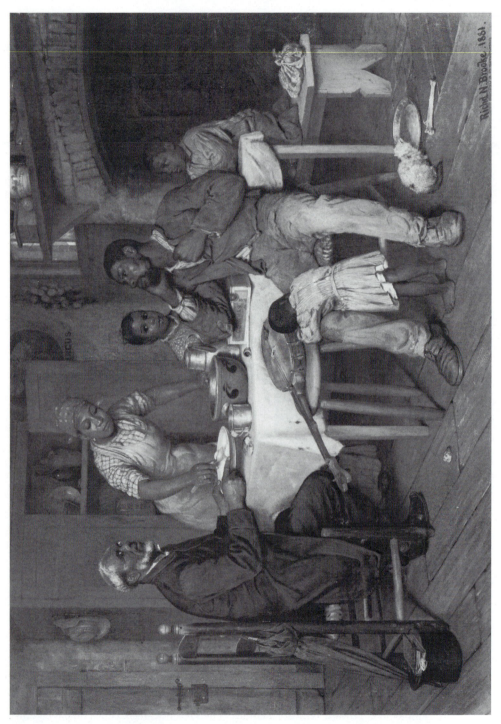

FIGURE 109. Richard Norris Brooke. "A Pastoral Visit, Virginia." 1881. Oil on canvas. 47¾ × 65¾ in. Collection of the Corcoran Gallery of Art. Museum purchase, Gallery Fund, 81.8. Washington, D.C.

FIGURE 110. J. Wells Champney. "Negro Prayer Meeting." 1874. Wood engraving, mixed media. Published in "Southern Mountain Rambles," by Edward King. *Scribner's Monthly* 8 (1874).

The settings of these pictures are vague, depicting mostly simple wooden tables on raised platforms, behind which the preacher stands; it is obvious that the artists want to focus viewer attention on the personality of the preachers, brushing aside extraneous matters. Finally, however, it is the passion of the preacher's oratory that commands the attention of his congregation—and, of course, that of the viewer—and this theme is reinforced by the artist's use of motifs that further identify the preacher's uniqueness.

There is his omnipresent Bible, placed in the center of the picture, or near the center, which lies open to a page that he might consult at any moment. Indeed, he often points to words on the page as he preaches. The importance of the Bible in the culture of the black community cannot be overstated, for not only is it the source of God's Word, it is also a reminder to the congregation that the preacher, being literate, is the transmitter of the Word to his people. Indeed, Reinhart's "colored preacher" has two Bibles (fig. 93): one he holds in his hands, and the other rests before him on a large, ornate, tasseled pillow.

Typically, artists portray the black preacher as elderly with white or gray hair and beard, or as bald, or nearly bald, with white puffs of hair at the sides, and often wearing eyeglasses. If a younger man, he is given an imposing stature, commanding presence, and distinctive style of dress. Old or youngish, the preacher wears a stovepipe hat, frock coat (however tattered), and clerical collar. When in the pulpit, he places his top hat conspicuously about the pulpit, on top of the podium, or on the floor beside it or on a chancel post behind it. The dandy types also wear white gloves and carry a cane, which are placed atop the hat before they begin to preach (fig. 104).

The preachers shown in figures 93–106 can be regarded as representative of the hundreds—no, thousands—of the ex-slave clergymen of the postbellum era who assumed leadership roles in the development of the emerging black church. The oratory style of the black preacher varies as much from one individual to the next as does his persona and the message he gives his listeners; indeed, one of the characteristic features of the black folk sermon is its unique individuality.

Some features of course are common to the oratory of the black folk preacher: the use of intonation or chant in delivering the prayers and parts of the sermon, the predilection for drawing upon the poetic language of the Bible, the continuous engagement of the congregation in a dialogue that takes the form of call-and-response performance, the use of timing as a device for controlling the pace of the sermon, and of pitch as a tension builder that assists the preacher in controlling the gradual movement from low and soft tones to the strident climax of the sermon.

Congregations encouraged the eccentricity of their pastors by accepting it with great enthusiasm—the mannerisms, peculiar use of the English language, and occasional unintelligibility. Worshipers were moved by the extravagant gestures and actions—when the preachers marched back and forth in the pulpit, leaped into the air, rose slowly on tiptoe while extending the arms over the head, clapped the hands and twirled around. These things can be represented in the painting or print; what cannot be conveyed pictorially is the fact that the black preacher as a type is a consummate storyteller who can hold his listeners mesmerized for hours at a time.

In 1904, writer Clifton Johnson described such a minister in his book *Highways and Byways of the South*. "To add fervor to his religious eloquence, he assumed a voice so hoarse and violent that his words were scarcely distinguishable. He had a rhythmic way of expelling four or five words in an explosive shout, and then drawing in his breath with a sudden rasping snort. This kind of delivery he continued all through [his sermon], except when he broke into a wail, or sang a line of a hymn. . . . Striding back and forth across the platform, he waved his arms and distorted his body. Sometimes he crouched low behind the pulpit almost out of sight. . . . The audience supplemented the preaching with an occasional 'Amen,' 'Glory be,' 'Yes, indeed.' "[3]

Of the three scenes that show a preacher addressing his congregation, two portray rural scenes—Alfred R. Waud's "Prayer-Meeting" and J. Campbell

Phillips's "The Gospel" (figs. 105 and 106)—and the other shows an urban church—David Hunter Strother's "The Negro Preacher" (fig. 104). Obviously poor, the rural congregations meet in a rude praise house and sit on rough benches, some without backs—all this reminiscent of plantation days—but they have dressed in their finest to attend the services, and they pay close attention to the words of the preachers. There is an intense, but decorous, tone to the services as the preachers approach the climactic points of their sermons.

The worship service under way at a middle-class church in Charleston, South Carolina (fig. 104), contrasts greatly to those of the rural churches. Here, too, the preacher addresses the congregation with great emotional fervor as he nears the climax of his sermon, but here the congregation supports him by calling out words of encouragement—"Praise the Lord," "Amen," "Glory, Glory," and the like. The eloquence of the sermon has moved some worshipers in the background to rise to their feet, and two women in the foreground appear to be calling out a hearty "Amen." This kind of musical dialogue between preacher and church members, typically found in the black folk church, never failed to fascinate white visitors, and many postbellum reports were published about the practice.

Sometimes it was the sheer novelty of the occasion that attracted wide attention; for example, the song services that took place on Sunday mornings in the African Church in Richmond, Virginia, moved a visiting journalist to try to describe what he heard:

> It is their custom to assemble about half an hour before the time of service and spend their time in singing their "spiritual songs." No one who has witnessed the scene can ever forget it. . . . People come in quietly and take their seats until the room is about half full. At this point (the congregation continuing to assemble) a low murmur is heard, at first hardly distinguishable from the rustling of incoming members. It proves to be a voice, but the ear fails to discern as yet a positive melody. It gradually becomes more distinct, and as it does so, a soft beating sound is heard in various parts of the room. It is from the feet of merry "worshippers," who thus respond to the rhythmic flow before they are fully prepared to join with their voices. But these are soon added, and the tide of song rises and falls with ever-varying solo and chorus, strophe and antistrophe, unison singing and part-singing, till the self-appointed leader becomes weary, or reaches the end of his list of verses, or for whatever reason he concludes to stop. A brief interval of silence then ensues, after which we hear another murmur, and the same experience is repeated.[4]

Although the songs of the slaves, and their style of singing those songs, were the subject of hundreds of literary pieces published in the nineteenth century, surprisingly few pictorial representations of slaves, or ex-slaves, have been discovered that show them solely occupied in singing. To be sure, everyone knew that African-Americans sang all the day, and all the night if so inclined, but always the singing served a specific purpose and was in the service of some major activity—worshiping God, burying their dead, dancing, working in the fields, and so on. Consequently, Howard Helmick's drawing of a large group of singers, "Plantation Slave Singers" (fig. 129), is exceptional. The viewer has to draw upon his or her own experience in order to imagine the sound of the singing, judging by the wide-open mouths of the singers, their distinctive posture, and enthusiastic hand-clapping.

A playbill that advertises the forthcoming concert of the "Sheppard's Jubilee Singers" (fig. 130) to be given in February 1875, stresses the humility of the slave singers and offers assurance that the program will consist of genuine old plantation songs. By implication, the message is sent that these singers are carriers of the authentic traditional music of the slaves, unlike such student groups as the popular Fisk Jubilee Singers and the Hampton Students, who, as trained musicians, no longer sang genuine black folk songs in the time-honored way.

Like many other literary figures of the time, poet Frances Gage found it difficult to explain why the singing of the ex-slaves was so affecting, though she believed the African-Americans to be a "thoroughly religious [and] mournful people," and therefore hardly to be expected to produce cheerful music (figs. 112–116). Their "moments of gaiety," she observes, suggest them to be full of fun, but it is only "on the surface" (fig. 116). During her travels in the Georgia Sea Islands in 1863, she reflects on the subject: "I have yet to hear them sing a light or merry song, although there is often mingled with their sadness a spirit of exaltation and faith that is truly touching. . . . Many of their melodies seem like a wail of anguish, as if a crushed soul was crying up to Jesus from the very depths of despair. They have their moments of gayety, when they seem to be all a-flutter with fun and frolic. But it is on the surface. Let that cease, and again the mournful current takes its way, and murmurs onward in a dull sluggish surge."[5]

Journalist Clarence Deming, writing in 1884, gives thought to the relationship between singing and religion:

> Half the joy in life of the negro of the Mississippi Bends is derived from vocal melody. . . . Music enters into every fibre of his being,—into his daily toil, his religion, his passions, his loves. But, while many of his songs are secular or even vicious, by far the larger part are those that pertain to worship. It may be said, indeed, that almost all his religion is a service of song. The preacher intones not a little of his sermon; the congregation accompany with a low melody during fully one-half the preacher's discourse; the prayers are often delivered to slow monotonous music by female voices; and actual intervals of the service are unknown,

for the intervals are filled by hymns, some of them so long that they give one a decided respect for the negro's powers of memory. . . .[6]

Joined in Christian Fellowship

To the ex-slaves the black church offered a variety of religious services that brought them together in forms of Christian association, of which the most important were of course the Sunday worship services and the prayer services held on week-nights; see, for example, "Negro Prayer Meeting" (fig. 110). Christians also met in religious fellowship when they gathered to observe rituals such as the sacraments of baptism, marriage, and death, and when some kinds of social activities provided opportunities for them to engage in religious exercises, such as, for example, the corn-shucking festival that ended with a prayer meeting. Finally, there was the annual revival meeting, which merged the various religious ceremonies, placing particular focus on prayer meetings and baptisms, and developing some of its own peculiar conventions, such as "seeking" and the "mourner's bench" (which will be discussed later, see pp. 139–41). While revivals might be held at any time of the year, the "big ones" generally took place in the late summer after crops had been "laid by."

The artists themselves differentiate among the various portrayals of informal worship services in our collection (figs. 110–117) by giving them dissimiliar titles: two are labeled "prayer meetings," two are "revival meetings," one is a "watch meeting," one is a "camp meeting," and two have no titles but do carry explanatory captions. Essentially, however, the meetings are alike: all the scenes depict African-Americans engaging in an unorthodox religious behavior that both appalled and entranced eyewitnesses, who saw some worshipers totally possessed by the Holy Spirit, while others were singing loudly, moaning, murmuring, shreiking, crying out, praying aloud, clapping their hands, waving their arms about, and generally giving evidence of being in a state of ecstatic seizure.

Black sociologist W. E. B. Du Bois was one of many observers who tried to describe this phenomenon for their readers. "Those who have not thus witnessed the frenzy of a Negro revival in the untouched backwoods of the South," he states, "can but dimly realize the religious feeling of the slave; as described, such scenes appear grotesque and funny, but as seen they are 'awful.' " Identifying the frenzy with shouting, he observes that it occurred "when the Spirit of the Lord passed by, and, seizing the devotee, made him mad with supernatural joy. . . ."[7]

Several of the images presented here depict a revivalistic theme: the sinner becomes converted, is baptized, and is welcomed into membership of the church, but first he must endure a period of trial and tribulation, which may last for some time. The revival-meeting theme was extremely popular with artists of the time, and of the several motifs associated with the theme, that of the "seeker" surely is the most colorful, whether he or she is depicted alone in coping with problems (fig. 125), is shown experiencing a heavenly vision (fig. 126), or is one of several sinners lying prostrate at the "mourner's bench" (fig. 115).

In 1873, correspondent A. L. Ingle Bassett described the kind of experience the sinner must undergo once he embarks upon the special, and lonely, mission to "find dat t'ing" and starts down the road to conversion. The penitent changes into a different person, as in "Seeking" (fig. 125). Having become a "seeker" or "mourner," he "assumes at once an air of abject wretchedness; a smile never parts the lips, and the song which once issued so constantly and joyously from them . . . is heard no more; occasionally, perhaps, a dirge-like chant, half-whispered takes the place of the song."[8] He moves with "bent head and listless step," speaking only when necessary. This overwhelming melancholy might last a few days or as long as several months. When his lengthy ordeal at last is over, he joyously informs his congregation that he has "come through," that he has "found de Lord," and wants to share with them his experiences.

The revival services portrayed in "A Negro Revival Meeting" (fig. 113) and "Shout, Sisters!" (fig. 115) show "seekers" who have been visited by the Holy Spirit during a worship service and have made their way up to the "mourner's bench" or "anxious seat"; the singing and praying of the congregation continues unabated, though some of the worshipers go to the assistance of the "seekers." In the final act of this mini-drama, those who have "come through" return to their local congregations, prepared to share their experiences with their fellow Christians, to submit to examination by the preacher and elders, to become candidates for baptism, and finally to be taken into the church as bona-fide members.

The anonymous eyewitness who published the short piece, "Colored Revivals in Virginia," which described a revival service he had attended, asserted that the illustration for this piece, "Scene at a Colored Revival Meeting" (fig. 114), was a "true and graphic picture of African worship in 'protracted meetings' in Virginia, and through the South generally."[9] Noting that the revival season was at its height, he marveled that people would walk long distances, four or five miles, to attend the nightly meetings, and that some would attend three times a day. At the beginning of the "protracted meeting" discussed above (fig. 114), four preachers were officiating—exhorting, praying, and singing—in "orthodox and reverential manner." Then a radical change took place. The worshipers had reached that stage of the proceedings where all attention was concentrated on the mourners, who had come up at intervals to the "bench" and were bowed down before the preacher's desk—men, women, boys, all mixed together, heads turned in. Around them and among them were the elder brethren, whispering encouragement, exhorting them, telling their own experience. . . . Meanwhile the preacher was shouting himself hoarse to the [other] mourners and spectators . . . but scarcely making himself heard above the din made by the congregation."[10]

The service would last for hours, with other mourners moving up to the "bench" through the long night and reporting on their ecstatic experiences. When a sizable number of converts had "come through," a time was set for their baptism.

Two of the artworks (figs. 111 and 112) depicting worship services represent historical events associated with the earthquake of August 1886, which devastated Charleston, South Carolina, and, because of its continuous eruptions, forced the citizenry to camp out in the city parks and private green places for

FIGURE 111. William Allen Rogers. "But There Sudden [*sic*] Rose among Them One of Earth's Untutored Kings." Wood engraving. Published in *City Legends,* by Will Carleton. New York: Harper and Brothers, 1890.

FIGURE 112. William Allen Rogers. "Negro Prayer-Meeting." Wood engraving, based on sketches by Frederic Remington, A. J. Gustin, and Willard Poinsette Snyder. Published in "Negro Prayer-Meeting. After the Earthquake at Charleston." *Harper's Weekly* 30 (1886).

FIGURE 113. William Ludlow Sheppard. "The Sunny South.—A Negro Revival Meeting—A Seeker 'Getting Religion.' " Wood engraving. Published in "Religion in the South. A Negro Revival in Virginia," by A. L. Ingle Bassett. *Frank Leslie's Illustrated Weekly Newspaper* 36 (1873).

FIGURE 114. Carter N. Berkeley. "Virginia—Scene at a Colored Revival Meeting— 'Oh! Come Down from Heben, en Ride Roun' in de Hearts uv des Sinners.' " Wood engraving. Published in "Colored Revivals in Virginia." *Frank Leslie's Illustrated Weekly Newspaper* 61 (1885).

FIGURE 115. "Shout, Sisters!" Pen and ink. Published in "Inside Southern Cabins. Georgia.—II." *Harper's Weekly* 24 (1880).

FIGURE 118. Howard Helmick. "Uncle Aaron's Advice from the Pulpit." Pen and ink. Published in *The Story of My Life*, by Mary A. Livermore. Hartford, Connecticut: A. D. Worthington and Company, 1897.

The worshipers gather early in the barn-like praise house, or local schoolhouse if no meeting-house is available, and begin to sing hymns, which are followed by exhortations, then hymns, and more hymns. As midnight approaches, the worshipers gradually grow quiet until there is absolute silence. With the striking of the hour, the whole scene changes.

Everybody becomes intensely animated . . . everybody congratulates everybody else. Then a hymn to a merry tune is given out, to which the watchers respond not only by their voices, but by their feet and hands, and until all are in motion—head-wagging, hand-shaking, body contortioning, foot-moving. There is laughing and singing and excitement. The old year has been watched out and the new year watched in.[11]

FIGURE 119. James Henry Moser. "Read er Chapter fer de Ederfurkashun of de 'Sembled Sinners." Wood engraving. Published in *Bright Days on the Old Plantation,* by Mary Ross Banks. Boston: Lee and Shepard Publishers, 1882.

FIGURE 120. Edward Potthast. "Brother Lazarus, Des er Minute fo' Yer Fling dat Line." Ink wash. Published in *Century Magazine* 58 (1899).

FIGURE 121. Edward Windsor Kemble. "Round, Round They Go." 1895. Crayon. Published in "A Black Settlement," by Martha McCulloch-Williams. *Harper's New Monthly Magazine* 93 (1896).

FIGURE 122. Edward Windsor Kemble. "Oh, Shoutin's Mighty Sweet." Pen and ink. Published in *Plantation Songs and Other Verses,* by Ruth M. Stuart. New York: D. Appleton and Company, 1916.

FIGURE 123. [Modern Shout.] Early 20th–c. Photograph. Published in *Slave Songs of the Georgia Sea Islands*, by Lydia Parrish. New York: Creative Age Press, 1942.

FIGURE 124. Alfred T. Bricher. "Religious Dancing of Blacks, Termed Shouting." Engraving by either Alban J. Conant or Bricher and Conant. Published in *The Black Man of the South and the Rebels,* by Charles Stearns. New York: American News Company, 1892.

FIGURE 125. William Ludlow Sheppard. "Seeking." Wood engraving by John Filver. Published in "Southern Sketches—IV." *Appleton's Journal of Popular Literature, Science, and Art* 4 (1870).

FIGURE 126. James Henry Moser. "Big Liz's Dream." Wood engraving. Published in *Bright Days in the Old Plantation Time*, by Mary Ross Banks. Boston: Lee and Shepard, 1882.

Camp Meetings and Bush Meetings

Possibly the most popular of all religious meetings among black folk in the nineteenth century was the camp meeting, which, as an institution, evolved during the Second Awakening, a Protestant revivalist movement beginning in the 1780s that swept over the United States and flourished until the 1830s. Its format was that of a gigantic religious service held in the woods, where the worshipers lived in tents for several days, sometimes as long as a week or more. The historic first camp meetings took place in July 1799 in forests and groves of Logan County, Kentucky; from there the movement quickly spread to other frontier states, then throughout the nation.

From the beginning, blacks constituted a large proportion of the participants: although segregated on the camp grounds, they listened to the preaching and joined in the singing, and on rare occasions black preachers were allowed to preach. Many descriptions of this uniquely American experience were published during the nineteenth century; some tourists, particularly among the European travelers, found the camp meeting intriguing, others found it offensive, and yet others found it degrading.

In about 1818, blacks began to leave the white-directed camp meetings to set up their own, which ranged in size from small groups composed of a few congregations that had banded together to organize a meeting, to immense gatherings of thousands, including both blacks and whites under black leadership, that drew campers from miles around. In the antebellum South, some slaveholders permitted their slaves to leave the plantation to attend camp meetings or bush meetings (that is, meetings without tents), and of course after Emancipation the ex-slaves were free to worship as they pleased.

Camp-meeting themes appealed not only to those artists in search of the sensational but also to those curious about the mystery associated with religious practices of the ex-slaves. The word-picture that follows could easily serve as a description of the camp meeting pictured in "A Negro Camp-Meeting in the South" (fig. 117) insofar as mood and effect upon the viewer are concerned, although picture and text are separated in time. Eben Rexford, reaching back into the past to recall the first time he went to a camp meeting, observes:

At camp-meetings and similar occasions, the negro gives himself up most fully to the musical abandon of the time and scene. Once [you] hear a revival hymn sung by a score of strong, rich voices, and you will never forget. I well remember when I first heard the following:

Dar's a low, sweet music,
Dar's a low. sweet music,
Dar's a low, sweet music,
From de ol' church yard

I hear de grave-stones breakin'
I hear de grave-stones breakin'
I hear de grave-stones breakin'
In de ol' church yard

I hear de Lord a callin'
I hear de Lord a callin'
I hear de Lord a callin'
From de ol' church yard.

Dar's a home I'se a gwine to,
Dar's a home I'se a gwine to,
Dar's a home I'se a gwine to,
From de ol' church yard.

To this day I have only to shut my eyes, and I see it all—the blazing heaps of pitchwood whose lurid light shone through the trees only a little distance, making the shadows beyond seem blacker by the contrast, the dusky faces of the singers lighted up with a strange excitement as they sang, keeping time to the slow mournful strains, with rhythmic movements of head and body. . . . Of all the songs heard at the South, I know of none whose melody surpasses that of this one, deep and solemn, with minor strains in it that merge into the majesty of a triumphal pean [*sic*]. . . .[12]

Writer-poet John Bennett, in transcribing a revival sermon he heard at a camp meeting, tries to convey some idea of how the singing contributes to the overall mystical tone of the service. As he walked down the road toward the church where the revival service would take place, he became aware of members of the congregation also moving along the road in the "shadowy darkness," singing softly "as wild airs as ever African twilight listened to," and seeming a part of it,

their bodies swaying from side to side, hands upraised, with harsh clapping sounds, their feet scarcely clearing the sandy ruts, shuffling, scuffling along, in time to the beat of their music. . . . As we paused at the edge of the little grove, a man with a wonderfully soft, deep voice was praying. He seemed almost to be singing, his voice was so melodious and so evenly modulated in its tones; a bass, . . . deep and suave as an organpipe . . . Suddenly, without a pause, and "where" I could not lay my finger, the chanted prayer turned into a song. The same deep voice led it. The others, with scarcely a moment's hesitation, joined in its quaint refrain . . . The voices all were bass, or baritones, of a rather somber cast, and all possessed the same searching, melancholy tone.[13]

The Ring Shout

One of the most exotic features of African-American religious practice is the holy dance called "the shout" (or "ring shout"), shown in Kemble's "Round, Round They Go" (fig. 121), the anonymous photograph of an early-twentieth-century shout (fig. 123), and Alfred T. Bricher's "Religious Dancing of Blacks, Termed Shouting" (fig. 124). Kemble's image of a single figure, "Oh, Shoutin's Mighty Sweet" (fig. 122), focuses on one of the participants in the ring. The origin of the shout reaches back to Africa, and the continuous influx of Africans into the United States during the first half of the nineteenth century—this despite the Act abolishing the slave trade that went into effect on January 1, 1808—insured that the tradition would be enriched rather than weakened over time.

The first references in print to the shout, which date from the early 1800s in the United States, suggest it to be a rather simple dance, much like the ring dances the European explorers saw in West Africa in the eighteenth and early nineteenth centuries.[14] One of the earliest comments on the dance comes from Methodist clergyman John F. Watson, of Philadelphia, who complains in 1819 that at camp meetings "the coloured people get together, and sing for hours together" songs that are a "discredit" to Christianity. Worse yet, as he notes with obvious impatience, they were engaging in an activity that was remarkably similar to actual dancing: "with every word so sung, they have a sinking of one or other leg of the body alternately; producing an audible sound of the feet at every step, and as manifest as the steps of actual negro dancing in Virginia . . . ," while those who sit on the sidelines "strike the sounds alternately on each thigh."[15]

Obviously, this presumably holy exercise is simply the African ring dance, for which the bystanders provide accompaniment by singing and pattin' Juba. After converting to Christianity, the blacks had to give up dancing, along with other "sinful things," but the ring-dance tradition was too strong to be easily discarded. Not surprisingly, the early black Christians sublimated it into a holy dance. The only essential differences between the pagan ring and the Christian holy ring were that in performing the latter the shouter must not cross the feet and should sing "spiritual songs."

Novelist Frederika Bremer was only one of many observers who came away from a camp meeting feeling that the holy dance of the black worshipers differed little from one of their plantation frolics. In May 1850 she visited a camp meeting in progress near Charleston, South Carolina, and remained through the next day:

It was now past midnight; the weather had cleared, and the air was so delicious and the spectacle so beautiful that I was compelled to return to the tent to tell Mrs. Howland, who at once resolved to come out with me . . . We went the round of the camp, especially on the black side. And here all the tents were still full of religious exaltation, each separate tent presenting some new phases. . . . We saw in one [tent] a zealous convert . . . surrounded by devout auditors; in another we saw a whole crowd of black people on their knees, all dressed in white . . . in a third women were dancing the holy dance for one of the newly converted. This dancing, however, having been forbidden by the preachers, ceased immediately upon our entering the tent. I saw merely a rocking movement of women, who held each other by the hand in a circle, singing the while.[16]

Some of the literary descriptions of the postbellum shout refer to dances that can be very elaborate, varying in detail from one place to another and carrying different names from one region to another, of which the most common were: "Rockin' Daniel," "Stomping on de Old Boy," "Marching 'Round Jericho," "the Dead March," and "the Glory Shout." No matter how complicated the dance, however, the basic elements remain the same.

The shout takes place only *after* formal services on Sundays or at prayer meetings during the week. If held inside the praise house, the benches are pushed back against the wall, and the shouters begin walking single file in circle formation around the room, at first slowly, then gradually faster and faster, while moving into a shuffle step with bent knees and barely lifting the feet from the floor. Generally some of them begin to sing as they proceed, and three or four persons standing to the side give support by singing, foot-stomping, and clapping hands, together or on the knees.

A shout might last for hours, the shouters stopping to rest only for brief intervals between the verses of the songs or when dropping out of the circle at the point of exhaustion, then returning when rested. At the end of each verse, the shouters stop short, stomp, then begin dancing with the other foot forward. Shouters might shout the same song twenty or thirty times in this manner before changing to another one.

Kemble's "Round, Round They Go" (fig. 121) and "Oh, Shoutin's Mighty Sweet" (fig. 122) depict the simple ring shout. The artist's drawings capture perfectly the momentum of the shouters' movement around the room, their ecstatic mood, and especially the joy of their singing. His image of the solo shouter (fig. 122) also is informative. The anonymous photographer, working under difficult constraints, nevertheless succeeds in snapping his or her picture at just the right moment and also captures the ring–shout dancers in motion. (fig. 123).

In contrast, Bricher's shout, "Religious Dancing of the Blacks, Termed Shouting" (fig. 124), illustrates how raucous a performance can become. His shouters have formed a ring and are shuffling around the room with uninhibited jollity and abandon, singing loudly as they move, some waving outstretched arms in the air. Some also may be screaming and moaning, several are clapping their hands, and at least one male shouter in the foreground center appears to be pattin' Juba. Two or three of the shouters have abandoned the shuffle step, are lifting their feet off the floor, and one woman, just off center of the drawing, clearly has been possessed by the Holy Spirit and is jumping high in the air.

The special songs of the shouters attracted as much attention as did the dancing. In 1867, an eyewitness wrote: "The voices of the colored people have a peculiar quality that nothing can imitate . . . the intonations and delicate variations of even one singer cannot be reproduced on paper. And I despair of conveying any notion of the effect of a number singing together, especially in a complicated shout like 'I can't stay behind.' "[17] According to some ex-slave informants, the religious songs of the slaves fell into two categories, "sperichils" (spirituals) and "running sperichils" (shout songs), but actually any song might be used for shouting. Some spirituals became associated with shouting by long tradition and were widely disseminated, such as "Pray All de Member"; "De Bell Done Ring"; "Lawd, I Touch One String"; "O Shout, O Shout, O Shout Away."

Counselor to His Flock

After Emancipation, the black church began to evolve into the institution that would constitute the central core of African-American culture, even before the church, first, had outgrown the praise cabin and, later, the barn and, finally, the schoolhouse converted into a meeting place. In addition to serving as the religious center of the community, the black folk church, under the guidance of its preachers, would become also a social and civic center—a place where people could meet and discuss issues of mutual interest (figs. 118–120). The pastor's duties took him into the community on social errands as well as religious ones, to comfort the sick, counsel the depressed, and share Christian fellowship with his members, particularly as a dinner guest on Sundays (figs. 107–109).

The itinerant preacher represented in "Rev. Ezekial Moses" (figs. 107 and 108) travels by mule to visit members of his congregation who live far out in the country. Perhaps he is visiting the sick (his Bible is tucked under his arm), or he has accepted an invitation to Sunday dinner. This is an important occasion for him, for his circuit is so far-flung that he can preach to each congregation only once a month, and he finds few opportunities for social contacts with his members. Obviously he is a sincere person and anxious to serve his ministry as best he can, though he is hardly overpaid for his services.

Richard Brooke's painting "A Pastoral Visit" (fig. 109), which depicts a moment in the "Sunday" everyday life of ex-slaves, refers to several themes at the same reading. Two motifs are immediately apparent: the domestic-scene motif, which shows the family gathered around the table in preparation for the Sunday dinner, and the music-making motif, represented by the large banjo in the center foreground of the picture. These merge with the themes of the religiosity of the black man and the importance of the black preacher. All members of the family, children as well as adults, hang on to each word the preacher speaks; the love and respect they have for him is almost palpable. And in a different sense, so is their love of music, which is essential for their survival. Oral tradition informs us that after dinner the father surely will pick up his banjo and entertain his preacher-guest with some favorite old hymn tunes and spirituals, and the others surely will join in singing the choruses.

Learning to Read

Another subject explored in postbellum artworks is the importance of education. As during the slavery era, education is to be obtained by any means possible, at any cost necessary. Winslow Homer's "Sunday Morning in Virginia" (fig. 127) and the anonymous photograph "I Would Like to Read a Sweet Story of Old" (fig. 128) show how teaching and learning reach into the lives of the young and elderly as well as those of the school-age population (compare antebellum figs. 27 and 28). The use of the Bible as a motif, given prominence by its off-center foreground position in figures 127 and 128 and the fact that it is the focal point of the eyes of all the figures except the old woman (who listens though her head is turned away), is again a reference to the theme of the religiosity of black folk—and a reminder that the Bible was the first primer of the slaves.

Rituals and Ceremonies

After the War, some of the artists who previously had developed an interest in constructing images of the slaves now turned to the communities peopled by the ex-slaves in search of themes that could be represented in artworks. For some of the artists, the weddings, baptismal ceremonies, and funeral/burial rites of African-Americans offered exotica that simply could be found in no other segment of American society. Moreover, the public, too, displayed curiosity about the cultural habits of the nation's newest citizens, but at the same time felt a nostalgic longing for the "good ole days befo' de war." Consequently, postbellum artworks often represent slavery themes, although the scenes, using ex-slaves as models, were produced after Emancipation.

FIGURE 127. Winslow Homer. "Sunday Morning in Virginia." 1877. Oil on canvas. 17¾ × 23⅔ in. Cincinnati Art Museum, John J. Emery Endowment (acc. no. 1924.247). Cincinnati, Ohio.

FIGURE 128. "I Would Like to Read a Sweet Story of Old." Photograph. Published in *Southern Workman* 37 (1907).

FIGURE 129. Howard Helmick. "Plantation Slave Singers." Pen and ink. Published in *The Story of My Life*, by Mary A. Livermore. Hartford, Connecticut: A. D. Worthington and Company, 1897.

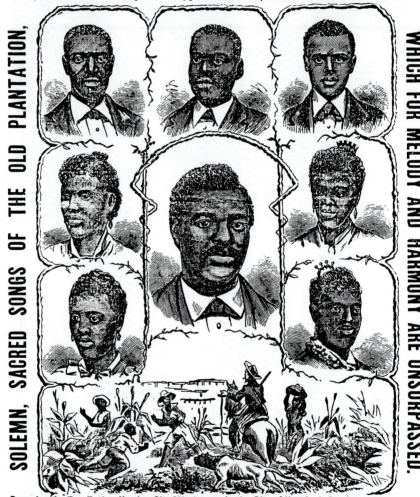

FIGURE 130. "Sheppard's Jubilee Singers." 1870s. Playbill. Pen and ink. Howard University, Moorland-Spingarn Collection. Washington, D.C.

FIGURE 131. Howard Helmick. "The Broomstick Wedding." Pen and ink. Published in *The Story of My Life,* by Mary A. Livermore. Hartford, Connecticut: A. D. Worthington and Company, 1897.

Wedding Ceremonies

Figures 131 to 136 represent three kinds of plantation wedding scenes, which, although produced by artists after the Civil War, purport to portray slave weddings. Traditionally, the plantation wedding ceremonies comprise three phases: the observance of the marriage rites and rituals in a praise cabin or a room in the master's Big House; the procession of the bridal party to the place where the festivities will be held; and the feasting and dancing that conclude the evening, which might take place in the Big House or the slave quarters or in a clearing under the trees. To be sure, few slaves could look forward to the luxury of having so elaborate a wedding, but the conventions were established for those fortunate enough to be among them and, based on the evidence, emancipation brought few changes in these customs.

The presence of whites in pictures of African-American weddings is an anachronism, a throw-back to the times when some masters took special interest in the weddings of their favorite slaves and supervised the proceedings from beginning to end. After Emancipation, whites would hardly have been

FIGURE 132. Howard Helmick. "Giving the Bridal Couple a Good Send Off." Pen and ink. Published in *The Story of My Life,* by Mary A. Livermore. Hartford, Connecticut: A. D. Worthington and Company, 1897.

FIGURE 133. "The Ebony Bridal—Wedding Ceremony in the Cabin." Wood engraving. Published in "The Ebony Bridal," by Ella B. Washington. *Frank Leslie's Illustrated Weekly Newspaper* 32 (1871).

FIGURE 134. "The Ebony Bridal—Marching to the Feast." Wood engraving. Published in "The Ebony Bridal," by Ella B. Washington. *Frank Leslie's Illustrated Weekly Newspaper* 32 (1871).

present at an ex-slave wedding, or if so would hardly have been given a prominent position among the guests. The slavery system itself contributed to the hypocrisy attendant upon traditional slave weddings: all present knew that the minister could not close the ceremony with the phrases "What God hath joined together, let no man put asunder" or "Till death do you part," for the slaveholder had the right to sell slaves away from their spouses at any time.

The setting for "The Wedding, Long Ago" (fig. 136) is a shabby cabin with the slaveholder himself (or a minister?) conducting the service, the presence of the open Bible on a nearby table adding dignity to the proceedings. The bride, resplendent in her flowing white gown and headdress of orange blossoms and white veiling, and the groom, wearing a new frock coat, exchange vows as requested by the wedding celebrant, to the approval—apparently quite audible—of the few friends who are witnessing the affair.

Artist Howard Helmick employs two companion scenes to portray a "broomstick wedding," using the first scene, "The Broomstick Wedding" (fig. 131), to depict the ceremony, and the second, "Giving the Bridal Couple a Good Send Off" (fig. 132), to feature the procession. Though few in number, the

FIGURE 135. "The Ebony Bridal—The Ball." Wood engraving. Published in "The Ebony Bridal," by Ella B. Washington. *Frank Leslie's Illustrated Weekly Newspaper* 32 (1871).

wedding guests make up for their small numbers by their obvious enthusiasm, especially the musicians, who play violin, banjo, and large tambourine, accompanied by a boy energetically clapping his hands. The marriage ritual of jumping over a broom was an age-old slave custom, and there were many ways to perform it, depending upon the preacher or presiding dignitary, who called out instructions to the bride and groom—here assisted informally by the guests.

The third set of this group of wedding images depicts a grand affair, "The Ebony Bridal" (figs. 133–135), for which the anonymous artist uses three sequential scenes to tell the story. First, the black preacher is shown officiating at the ceremony, reading from a Bible (fig. 133); then the company marches to the barn-size cabin that will serve as a temporary ballroom (fig. 134); and finally we enter the ballroom itself (fig. 135), which is brilliantly lit for the occasion. The elaborate attire of the assembled company points up the elegance of the affair, and adds to the dignity of the occasion, particularly the white muslin dresses with décolleté necklines worn by the bride and her bridesmaids and their orange-blossom headdresses and garlands.

The artist highlights the important role of music in making this an affair of great importance. The typical plantation combination of banjo and fiddle, unacceptable for this affair, is replaced by the high-status ensemble of trumpet and cello. In all three scenes the musicians occupy prominent space, which automatically gives them the attention of the viewer and insures that the music will be "seen" as well as "heard."

Appropriately, the leading characters of this drama—foremost, the bride and groom—occupy the center middle ground of the ball scene, where they stand out against a background filled with a large, indeterminate number of guests, whom we notice not only because of their finery but also for their extravagant dancing, particularly among the men. The musicians frame the picture: on the right side the trumpeter and cellist are joined by a woman who claps her hands with great vigor, and on the left side is a woman enthusiastically pattin' Juba. Both male musicians are deeply engrossed in their playing: the cellist bends low over his instrument, oblivious to the noise around him, and the trumpeter, who has closed his eyes, frowns. Judging from the lively antics of the dancers and the intense concentration of the musicians, it appears that the gathered company is in for a wild but glorious night.

Baptism by Immersion

Without any doubt, the most spectacular, regularly recurring event in the black rural community was the baptismal ceremony. Large numbers of people, dressed in their finest clothes, came from miles around to watch it, ready to spend long hours in praying, listening to sermons, singing, and praising the Lord. By the late nineteenth century, the majority of black Christians were members of the Baptist Church, for whom baptism meant total immersion in the water rather than the "sprinkling" practiced by the other Protestant sects. A full gathering of a church's members and visitors at a baptism was a colorful affair, the female candidates in their white gowns and the men in white pants and shirts (or also in white gowns), with kerchiefs tied around their heads, offering sharp contrast to the onlookers attired in the colors of their Sunday finery.

Two of our drawings of baptismal services are set in rural areas. The "Pawson [sic] Demby" sketch (fig. 137), although intended to elicit a smile from the viewer, nevertheless includes the essential motifs that indicate a baptismal ceremony—a serious affair—is under way. In the center of the picture are the water, in this instance a hole broken into a frozen creek, and the preacher and his white-gowned candidate, who interact with each other. The small faithful group of church members shivering in the left background, who have come to watch the proceedings despite the cold, undoubtedly includes more candidates, for some of the women are robed in white. Several of the group are singing, and in the far distance a tiny church rises above snow-covered hills and a wooded area.

More commonly, baptismal services were attended by large numbers of persons, as depicted in "Baptizing in the Pool" (fig. 139). In the clearing of a woodland, in front of a church looming high in the upper-left background, an indeterminate number of church members and bystanders have gathered at poolside to watch the baptismal rites. The minister leads a white-gowned candidate into the water, which is almost waist deep, reciting the words of the ritual as he does so; lined up behind her are other candidates, male and female, also dressed in white. Everyone watches intently, most of them singing all the while—apparently with great enthusiasm, judging by their widely open mouths. In the background are horses and buggies, whose occupants are only now alighting, suggesting that they are late because they have come long distances. Also moving toward the gathered company are two latecomers who apparently have come a long way on foot.

Contemporary literature is replete with reports on the novelty of these observances of the baptism sacrament. Sometimes it was the patience of the candidates that moved observers to amazement, as a correspondent for the *Independent* noted in 1862:

> A few days ago there was a public administration of baptism on Ladies Island, opposite Beaufort [South Carolina], when thirty-four candidates were baptized. It was an interesting scene. Upon the beach were groups of negroes in their holiday attire; and from either side of the beach, for half a mile, others were moving toward the spot. The candidates were by themselves, in single file, ready to be conducted into the water.

FIGURE 136. "The Wedding, Long Ago." Pen and ink. Published in *A Golden Wedding and Other Tales,* by Ruth McEnery Stuart. New York: Harper and Brothers, 1893.

FIGURE 137. "Jes Gib Huh An-nubba Dip, Pawson Demby." Pen and ink. Published in *Ole Mars an' Ole Miss,* by Edmund K. Goldsborough. Washington, D.C.: National Publishing Company, 1900.

FIGURE 140. Alfred Kappes. "The Funeral." Wood engraving. Published in "The Funeral," by Will Carleton. *Harper's Weekly* 30 (1886).

late summer after the crops had been harvested and before the beginning of cotton-picking time, a carryover from slavery days when that season of the year offered some respite from plantation toil, and slaveholders were inclined to give their workers time off. Often the special funeral services were held under the umbrella of the church's annual revival meetings (see also p. 51–53).

Notes

1. Clarke, "A Call," 28.
2. Du Bois, *Souls,* Chapter 10.
3. Johnson, *Highways,* 57.
4. "Waifs," 273.
5. Gage, "Religious Exercises," 6.
6. Deming, *By-Ways,* 370.
7. Du Bois, *Souls,* Chapter 10.
8. Bassett, "Negro Revival," 346.
9. "Colored Revivals," 56.
10. Ibid.
11. "Virginia Watch," 351.
12. Rexford, "Negro Music," 85.
13. Bennett, "Revival Sermon," 257.
14. Southern, *Music,* 20.
15. Watson, *Methodist Error,* 29
16. Bremer, *Homes,* 158.
17. Allen, *Slave Songs,* iv–v.
18. "Baptist," 3.
19. "A Scene from Richmond," 1.
20. Bassett, "Negro Revival," 346.

Everyday Life
after Emancipation

After the War, many of America's wartime artists turned to the painting of rural scenes, particularly "farm life"—some in response to the nostalgia for the good old days that enveloped the nation at the time, and others because they were ready to embrace something different after several years of depicting war scenes. Insofar as the ex-slaves were concerned, "farm life" was a euphemism for plantation life and its slave culture. Whereas artists might have found themselves in unfamiliar territory in attempting to work out ways to represent the emergent black church and related issues—as is evident by the kinds of pictures they produced—the artists met few problems in constructing images of black laborers on the farms and plantations in the South. Using the same subjects in depicting black laborers as they used for whites, artists produced paintings and prints of card players, corn-husking bees, country weddings, dancers, longshoremen, musicians, and street vendors. The differences, however, between black and white worker scenes are striking, primarily because the ex-slave scenes reveal the strength and tenacity of African elements in the slave culture.

Songs of the Workers

Our collection includes thirty-six pictures representing black laborers in the postbellum era engaged in music-making as they work—or, at the end of the workday. Artists portray them on farms and plantations, working at various tasks at various times of the workday: men and children blowing horns or ringing the plantation bell at dawn to rouse their fellow workers (figs. 141–144); the hunter signaling the start of the hunt (fig. 145); women attending to their domestic chores (figs. 146–147); women and children cradling babies (figs. 148–151); and men and women working in the fields (figs. 152–160). Representing those workers who have left the plantation are images of factory hands (figs. 161–166), fishermen (fig. 167), river men (figs. 168 and 169), and street vendors (figs. 170–176).

The thematic link among these scenes is the importance of functional music for black workers. In common with many other peasant peoples, the slaves developed an extensive repertory of simple songs that served specific functions in their everyday lives. Harris Barrett, a black graduate of Hampton

FIGURE 141. Alfred R. Waud. "The Call to Labor." Wood engraving. Published in "Scenes on a Cotton Plantation." *Harper's Weekly* 11 (1867).

FIGURE 142. Edward Windsor Kemble. "The Breakfast Horn." Pen and ink. Published in *The Adventures of Huckleberry Finn (Tom Sawyer's Comrade),* by Mark Twain. New York: Harper and Brothers, 1897.

Institute, writing in 1912 about the folksongs of his people, observes that the songs fall into four categories: religious songs or spirituals, cradle songs, labor songs, and dance and game songs.[1]

He distinguishes between the labor songs, in which the singers "keep time with their work, the time of the music regulating the rapidity of the work," and those songs that simply are "rousing and inspiring" to sing while working. The former can be heard throughout the South, he notes, particularly where men work on wharves or railroads or other kinds of public works:

It is exceedingly interesting to watch a gang of men employed in digging a road bed. At a distance it is noticeable that the rise and fall of their picks is as regular and exact as the movement of a company of well-drilled soldiers. Upon closer approach there is heard a monotonous recitative— half chant, half conversation—and it is to the time of this song, if song it can be called, that the men work in such perfect unison. For hours at a time they keep this up, and though the sun may be shining with tropical fierceness, seldom is a man seen to lose time or to drop out until the leader ceases his song.[2]

FIGURE 143. Edward Windsor Kemble. "The Plough-Hands' Song (Jasper County—1860)." Pen and ink. Published in *The Tar Baby and Other Rhymes of Uncle Remus,* by Joel Chandler Harris. New York: D. Appleton and Company, 1904.

THE PLANTATION-BELL.

FIGURE 144. Edward Windsor Kemble. "The Plantation-Bell." Pen and ink. Published in *330 Drawings by Edward Windsor Kemble,* collected and arranged by Newton Chisneil. Brooklyn, New York: n.p., 1896.

The second class of labor songs—to be heard in the tobacco factories; on the cotton, rice, and sugar plantations; and at the corn-shucking festivals—calls for a talented song leader, who improvises the verses of the songs as he sings and brings the other workers in on the choruses. This class also includes those who sing to themselves, as pictured in "So Wid My Hoe I Go" (fig. 152).

Black workers, with their propensity for using whatever materials are at hand to make musical instruments—another form of improvising—fashioned signaling and announcing instruments from the horns of animals, as shown in "The Call to Labor" (fig. 141), "The Breakfast Horn" (fig. 142), "The Plough-Hands' Song" (fig. 143), and "The Hunting Song" (fig. 145). They also pressed into service the long straight bugles, five to six feet in length and made of tin or wood, as depicted in "Old Gabe" (fig. 162) and "The Summons to a Tobacco Sale" (fig. 163, see further about the bugles on pp. 190–91). And of course bells, too, function as signaling instruments, both the large outdoor type shown in "The Plantation-Bell" (fig. 144) and the small handbell in "The Auctioneer's Young Man" (fig. 161).

FIGURE 145. Hampton Institute Camera Club. "The Hunting Song—Rural South." Photograph. Published in *Poems of Cabin and Field,* by Paul Laurence Dunbar. New York: Dodd, Mead, and Company, 1899.

The pictures depicting female ex-slaves singing as they go about their domestic chores bring to viewer attention the place of black women in the postbellum community, at least as seen through the eyes of white artists. The kinds of household tasks that occupy their time are pictured in "Mammy's Churning Song" (fig. 146) and "Yon Go dat Po' Grimshaw Gang" (fig. 147), but women of course also work in the fields alongside the men. Above all, there is the singer of lullabies, who might be a woman, as depicted in "By the Fireplace" (fig. 148) and "Daddy's Comin' Home" (fig. 149); or a young boy, as in "Hieronymus Sings a Soothing Ditty" (fig. 150); or a young girl, as in "A Lullaby" (fig. 151).

FIGURE 146. Edward Windsor Kemble. "Mammy's Churning Song." Pen and ink. Published in "Mammy's Churning Song," by Edward A. Oldham. *Century Magazine* 40 (1890).

FIGURE 147. James H. Moser. "Yon Go Dat Po' Grimshaw Gang, Movin' Ergin." 1881. Wood engraving. Published in *Bright Days in the Old Plantation Time,* by Mary Ross Banks. Boston: Lee and Shepard, 1882.

BY THE FIREPLACE.

FIGURE 148. Edward Potthast. "By the Fireplace." Charcoal and wash. Published in "Negro Spirituals," by Marion Alexander Haskell. *Century Magazine* 58 (1899).

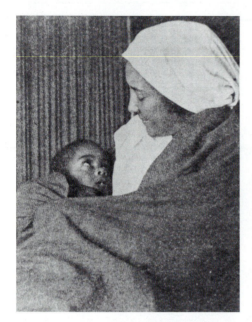

FIGURE 149. John Wesley Work. "Daddy's Comin' Home." Photograph. Published in *Folk Song of the American Negro*, by John Wesley Work. Nashville, Tennessee: Fisk University Press, 1915.

FIGURE 150. Arthur Burdett Frost. "Hieronymus Sings a Soothing Ditty." Mixed media. Published in "Hieronymus Pop and the Baby." *Harper's New Monthly Magazine* 61 (1880).

FIGURE 151. Rose Mueller. "A Lullaby." Wood engraving. Published in "Phrony Jane's Lawn Party," by Sydney Dayne. *Harper's Young People: An Illustrated Magazine* 3 (1882).

FIGURE 152. Edward Windsor Kemble. "So wid My Hoe I Go/Row on Row, Row on Row." Pen and ink. Published in *Plantation Songs and Other Verses,* by Ruth McEnery Stuart. New York: D. Appleton and Company, 1916.

FIGURE 153. "Picking the Nuts. Scenes and Incidents of a Southern Tour—Peanut-Culture on the Battlefield of Petersburg." Mixed media. Published in *Frank Leslie's Illustrated Weekly Newspaper* 61 (1885).

One of the most striking examples of functional music among the farm images is the group scene in "Picking the Nuts" (fig. 153), which shows a peanut-culture farm near Petersburg, Virginia, in 1885—striking because the banjoist, though dressed as a worker, obviously has the responsibility for providing entertainment music for the workers, who include women as well as men. There is no question that the music serves to coordinate the movements of the workers, for each works at his or her own pace; this is pleasure music, its purpose simply is to help move the work along as rapidly as possible. The banjoist sings with vigor and zest, but only one or two workers sing, which suggests that they are participating in a call-and-response performance, the former singing the verses and the other workers singing the choruses. During the slave era, good song leaders were in great demand, and the planters often were willing to pay top prices for them in the belief that they contributed to the economic well-being of the plantation by motivating the slaves to work harder.

Although the singing in the cotton-field scene, "The Field Hands Were Singing" (fig. 154), is less vigorous than among the tobacco-farm laborers, such scenes nevertheless were bizarre enough to attract the attention of tourists. In 1852 an English tourist in South Carolina noted, "While at work in the cotton fields, the slaves often sing some wild, simple melody by way of mutual cheer, which usually ends with a chorus, in which all join with a right hearty good will, in a key so loud as to be heard from one plantation to another.[3] The man in the left center of this picture, apparently the improvising song leader, sings loudly as he bends over to pluck a cotton boll to toss in his bag close at hand.

Corn-Shucking: Work and Play

One of the most popular subjects for postbellum artists was the corn-shucking festival (figs. 155–160), as indeed also had been the case in the antebellum era (compare figs. 46–48). Described again and again in contemporary nineteenth-century literature, the festivity had its own peculiar rituals, which varied from place to place, but generally comprised three phases: the march to the site where the corn husking would take place, the shucking of the corn, and the dance/feast afterward. The paintings constructed by artists that show whites making merry at corn-husking bees share very little in common with the scenes of black folk having a good time at their corn-shucking fetes, other than the fact that both types of representations use piles of corn ears as the starting point.[4]

Preparations get under way when the host begins to pile the corn in huge stacks in front of cribs or a barn, sets a date for the frolic, and sends invitations to farmers from all around. Before the War, the slaveholder would have been the host who would have sent invitations to his neighbors, and they in turn

FIGURE 154. Edward Windsor Kemble. "The Field Hands Were Singing As They Picked the Opening Cotton." Pen and ink. Published in *Daddy Jake the Runaway, and Short Stories Told After Dark by "Uncle Remus,"* by Joel Chandler Harris. New York: Century Company, 1896.

FIGURE 155. James Henry Moser. "Corn-Shucking Song." 1880. Wood engraving. Published in *Uncle Remus, His Songs and Sayings,* by Joel Chandler Harris. New York: D. Appleton and Company, 1893.

FIGURE 156. James Henry Moser. "Dat's de Lick, Little Ellick." Wood engraving. Published in *Bright Days in the Old Plantation Time,* by Mary Ross Banks. Boston: Lee and Shepard, 1882.

FIGURE 157. Howard Helmick. "A Plantation 'Corn-Shucking.' " Gouache. Published in *The Story of My Life*, by Mary A. Livermore. Hartford, Connecticut: A. D. Worthington & Company, 1897.

would have brought their slaves with them to the corn-shucking. After the War, any freedman might serve as a host.

On the day of the great event, guests begin arriving before nightfall, flooding the air with music as they march down the roads over hills and in valleys, some coming also by muleback or horseback, in wagons, and even by canoes—see James Henry Moser's "Corn-Shucking Song" (fig. 155). As new gangs meet those already on the roads, they, too, join in the singing, which can be heard for miles around, enriched by the sounds of homemade long bugles made of wood and the homemade quills blown by some of the men.[5] If there is no moon, the workers bring their pine-knot torches to light the way.

At the site, the gathered company chooses a song leader, called a General, who must possess a strong, rich voice and a talent for improvisation. Then the work begins. Keeping his huskers going fast and furiously, the General improvises verses about anything that comes to his mind and brings the workers in on the choruses of his songs. Moser's "Dats de Lick, Little Ellick" (fig. 156) and Arthur Burdett Frost's "The Corn-Shucking" (fig. 158) show the gathered workers in high spirits, organizing themselves and preparing their attack on the huge pile of corn.

Figure 158. Arthur Burdett Frost. "The Corn-Shucking." Wash. Published in *The Tar-Baby and Other Rhymes of Uncle Remus,* by Joel Chandler Harris. New York: D. Appleton and Company, 1904.

In some places, the host divides the corn pile into two equal parts by laying a fence rail across the top, and the two Generals compete against each other, as shown in Sheppard's "The Shucking" (fig. 159), or there are two piles of corn from the beginning, each with its own General. Singing and urging along the workers, the Generals stay atop the piles until victory is declared by one group or the other. In "Corn-Shucking Song" (fig. 155), the invited guests are beginning to assemble, coming in from the roads and from across the fields, but the General has not waited for them. Already he has begun the singing, using an ear of corn as his baton, and the workers are responding to his energetic gestures.

Although phase two of the festival typically is a vocal event, there is evidence that sometimes instrumentalists assisted the singers in keeping the momentum going. As pointed out earlier in the antebellum scene "Husking Corn" (fig. 46), the Leader/General plays a fiddle in addition to directing the singing of the six corn huskers, who sing lustily as they work. In Howard Helmick's postbellum "Plantation 'Corn-Shucking' " (fig. 157) a banjoist and a bones player assist the General in energizing the workers.

FIGURE 159. William Ludlow Sheppard. "The Shucking." Wood engraving. Published in "A Georgia Corn-Shucking," by David C. Barrow. *Century Magazine* 24 (1882).

Over the years a sizable repertory of corn-shucking songs was developed, carried from plantation to plantation throughout the South by slaves, freedmen, and tourists, with the result that collections can be found in a number of books and periodicals published in the nineteenth century. A widely distributed song used at the beginning of the corn husking was the following:

Here is yer corn-shucker Oh, ho ho ho ho,
Here is yer nigger ruler, Oh, ho ho ho ho
Don't yer hyer me holler? Oh, ho ho ho ho
Don't yer hyer me lumber? Oh, ho ho ho ho, Etc.[6]

An astonishing amount of work is accomplished at a corn-shucking owing to the excitement evoked by the singing and the rivalry of the huskers. When the piles are down to the last few ears of corn, the process of "rounding up" begins, and the workers sing a song such as the following, or one with similar text:

Round up, dubble up, round up corn
Round up, nubbins up, round up corn.[7]

After a successful conclusion to the husking, the workers are ready for the third phase—feasting, lots of horseplay, and, above all, dancing. William Ludlow Sheppard uses a diptych format in his scenes, showing first "The Shucking" (fig. 159), then "The Dance" (fig. 160). As is typical in the portrayal of black folk dance scenes, the artist presents very few dancers: featured are only one couple and a male soloist, who demonstrate the latest dance fads while an indeterminate number of workers watch intently, some of them singing heartily and at least one energetically clapping his hands. The musicians—a fiddler and a straw-beater—are pushed into the background of the picture, but because of their elevated position above the heads of the dancers, they easily attract the attention of the viewer.

The straw-beater, according to one visitor, need not be well trained: "any one can succeed, with proper caution, the first time he tries."[8] He needs only to select a pair of straws about eighteen inches in length from a sedge-broom, making sure they are "stout enough to stand a good smart blow," and, using them as drumsticks, beat on the bottom part of the fiddle-strings, the part between the fiddler's bow and his left hand. This noise of the straws, described as "tum tee tum," will still be heard after the dancers' feet have drowned out the sounds of the fiddler's music.

The corn-shucking fete was a plantation event that continued to flourish long after Emancipation, not only because it encouraged social interaction among the farmers but because it contributed to their developing ways to cooperate in undertaking large projects. Over the years, "members"—that is, farmers who had been converted to Christianity—replaced the dance-feast with a prayer meeting and feast.

FIGURE 160. William Ludlow Sheppard. "The Dance." Wood engraving by J. Clement. Published in "A Georgia Corn-Shucking," by David C. Barrow. *Century Magazine* 24 (1882).

FIGURE 161. James Wells Champney. "The Auctioneer's Young Man." Wood engraving. Published in "Glimpses of Texas," by Edward Smith King. *Scribner's Monthly Magazine* 7 (1874).

FIGURE 162. John Durkin. "Old Gabe."
Wood engraving. Published in "A Tobacco
'Break' at Lynchburg, Virginia." *Harper's
Weekly* 30 (1886).

FIGURE 163. James Wells Champney. "The
Summons to a Tobacco Sale." Mixed media.
Published in "A Ramble in Virginia: From
Bristol to the Sea," by Edward Smith King.
Scribner's Monthly Magazine 7 (1874).

Away from the Plantation

With an obvious interest in how the newly freed black folk would get along in
the competitive white world of the cities, away from the plantations, some
artists gave attention to portraying black men and women at labor. Workers
are shown on their way to work (figs. 167 and 168), amusing themselves during
breaks for lunch or dinner (figs. 164 and 166), and relaxing at the end of a hard
day (fig. 165), but we found very few pictures of freedmen actually singing as
they toiled at the work site—this, despite the fact that nineteenth-century literature is replete with word pictures of the freedmen toiling in the fields, chop-
ping down trees, stoking fires on the river steamers, rowing boats through the
lagoons and other inland waters, lifting bales of cotton on the wharfs, and so on.

In Virginia, one place to see, and hear, unusual music-making was at the
tobacco auctions, called "the breaks," where buglers used their homemade
instruments to announce the opening of the auction sales. The worker
depicted in "Old Gabe" (fig. 162)—Gabriel, a native of Lynchburg, Virginia—
was somewhat of a local celebrity for his ability to execute elaborate "fanfares"
on his long bugle.[9] A similar instrument appears in "The Summons to a

FIGURE 164. William Ludlow Sheppard. "Dinner-Time at the Tobacco-Factory." Wood engraving by John Filver. Published in "Southern Sketches—II." *Appleton's Journal of Popular Literature, Science, and Art* 4 (1870).

Tobacco Sale" (fig. 163). Both instruments reflect the influence of the African long-trumpet tradition on the makers of the long trumpets used on American plantations (see pp. 6, 176, 250–252).

Depicted in "The Fog Horn" (fig. 169) is another kind of horn put to use as a signaling instrument. At nightfall on St. John's River in Florida the air is filled with the "peculiar melodies" of the black crews as the small crafts that have been running the river all day tie up for the night. If a fog comes up, "the powerful note of the fog horn makes its way through the mists," drowning out the songs of the black roustabouts, and "guides the pilot to the point where a youthful African toils at the warning instrument."[10]

Finally, there is "The Auctioneer's Young Man" (fig. 161), which depicts a young advertiser who has successfully blended two kinds of improvised music, using his voice and his bell, to produce certainly a unique sound, more dissonant than consonant, which will attract attention to his message.

Scenes showing black factory workers dancing during the time allowed them for eating, "Dinner-Time at the Tobacco-Factory" (fig. 164) and "Courtyard of a Rice Mill" (fig. 166), refer to two themes that run throughout the

FIGURE 165. C. Upham. "Virginia—A Night Scene in Lynchburg during the Tobacco Season—Negro Tobacco Farmers Making Merry." Wood engraving. Published in *Frank Leslie's Illustrated Weekly Newspaper* 57 (1883).

collection: the importance of the dance in the lives of black folk, and the importance of teaching the young, who learn by emulation of, and encouragement from, adults. It is not acceptable simply to dance; one must be willing to invest the time necessary to become adept at it. The neophyte's peers watch his progress carefully and will make the final judgment of his skills.

"Song of the Oystermen" (fig. 167) shows fishermen of Annapolis, Maryland, on their way to work at Tally's Point Reef in Chesapeake Bay. Artist Joseph Becker, fascinated by their "melodious strains on a clear, autumnal

FIGURE 166. Georgiana Davis (?). "Courtyard of a Rice Mill. The Noon Hour." Mixed media. Published in "Georgia—The Cultivation of Rice—Work in the Field and Mill." *Frank Leslie's Illustrated Weekly Newspaper* 56 (1883).

morning, [which floated] across the tranquil waters of the bay," was inspired to make a sketch of the scene, and later used it as the basis for an engraving.[11] Accompanied by the banjo, the men sing the James Bland minstrel song "In de Evening by de Bright Light," which traditionally is sung in quartet style. The viewer assumes that these singers, too, are singing in quartet style, that the lead singer is the one on whom the artist has focused careful attention: his mouth is open very wide, and he stands tall above his seated companions in the left, mid-ground of the picture. Since the man on the far right is not singing, it is probable that the man whose back is to the viewer is the fourth member of the quartet—at least so his body position suggests.

"The Parting Song" (fig. 168) depicts a large number of "river men" singing one last song before the Mississippi River steamboat on which they work begins to leave port. Whether longshoremen, stevedores, roustabouts, or boat firemen, river men held a strange fascination for travelers, many of whom tried to describe in words the strange pull on the emotions they felt in the wild, weird songs of the river men.[12] It was traditional, especially at New Orleans, that the crew gather to sing as the flag was lowered, and it is this moment that artist A. R. Waud has caught. Two men stand at the top of the picture, the flag bearer and the song leader, but clearly it is the latter who is most important, commanding the immediate attention and admiration of the viewer; with feet spread wide and arm lifted high, he conducts the singing, appearing to be drawing every ounce of song from his men.

FIGURE 167. Joseph Becker. "Song of the Oystermen." Wood engraving. Published in "Maryland.—'In de Mornin' by de Bright Light.'—Negro Oystermen of Annapolis on Their Way to the Fishing-Ground in Chesapeake Bay." *Frank Leslie's Illustrated Weekly Newspaper* 51 (1880).

FIGURE 168. Alfred R. Waud. "Scene on a Mississippi Steamer—The Parting Song." Wood engraving. Published in *Harper's Weekly* 11 (1867).

River songs have a distinctive structure: each line of text improvised by the leader is followed by a refrain sung by the crew, which almost always consists of nonsense syllables and ends with a yell:

What boat is that, my darling honey
Oh ho, oh ho, ho, ah yah, yah ah!
She is the River Ruler, yes, my honey
Ah a—a-a-a yah a —ah! Etc.[13]

The singing might last for hours, depending upon the amount of work to be done; meanwhile, the leader will recite-sing improvised verses telling the history of the river, his personal history, the history of other river folk, and so on until the work is completed

For the ex-slaves, the preferred way to spend free time was in dancing, with or without instrumental accompaniment. A night scene in Lynchburg, Virginia, which shows tobacco famers relaxing before going to bed, features a dancer accompanied by a banjoist, a bones player, and a patter. All four men sing with great gusto, and the banjoist adds a percussive sound to the music

FIGURE 169. C. Upham. "The Fog Horn—St. John's River." Wood engraving. Published in Part 1 of "The New South—Scenes in North Carolina, Georgia and Florida." *Frank Leslie's Illustrated Weekly Newspaper* 56 (1883).

with his foot stomping. In the background a couple playing cards, watched by a third man, is unperturbed by the noise and the music. The dancer seems to be demonstrating the latest dance fad: his body is bent backward from the waist, one arm with dangling wrist lifted high over his head, and he balances on his toe. A young boy, keeper of the small open fire (bottom center of the picture), which lights up the faces of the music makers, is drinking in the scene, perhaps thinking about the time when he, too, will be able to play the banjo.

Street Vendors

Seven images of street vendors show them working the streets in both the North and the South, and the songs improvised by the vendors are as distinctive as their personalities, ages, and gender (figs. 170–176). A journalist writing about street cries of New York City notes, for example, that the vendors of hot corn, mostly colored women or girls, produced the most musical and characteristic cries, which were heard in the "still hours towards midnight. One of these strains, which had been chanted night after night, for several autumns past, by the same voice, in a central walk of the city, has a very wild and plaintive cadence. . . . After chanting this strain, the voice repeats the words 'hot corn' several times, in a short, jerking note; and then the plaintive little song is heard again, dying away in the distance."[14]

A few nineteenth-century vendors won a measure of celebrity for their street cries, among them the Hominy Man of Philadelphia (fig. 172) and the anonymous Strawberry Women of Charleston, South Carolina, whose song later was used in George Gershwin's opera, *Porgy and Bess*.[15]

FIGURE 170. "Beans and Potatoes." Mixed media. Published in "Inside Southern Cabins III.—Charleston, South Carolina." *Harper's Weekly* 34 (1880).

FIGURE 171. Benjamin West Clinedinst. "A Southern Oyster Peddler." Wood engraving. Published in *Harper's Weekly* 33 (1889).

FIGURE 172. William Ludlow Sheppard. "Old Hominy Man." Pen and ink. Published in *History of Philadelphia, 1609–1884,* by John Thomas Scharf and Thompson Westcott. Philadelphia: L. H. Everts and Company, 1884.

FIGURE 173. Edward Windsor Kemble. "A Marchande des Calas." Pen and ink. Published in *330 Drawings by Edward Windsor Kemble,* collected and arranged by Newton Chisneil. Brooklyn, New York: n.p., 1896.

FIGURE 174. Francis H. Schell. "Philadelphia Street Characters." Mixed media. Published in *Harper's Weekly* 20 (1876).

FIGURE 175. Frank H. Desch. "Spots! Git Yuh Fresh Spots!" Mixed media. Published in "In and About Old Hampton," by F. H. Desch. *Booklover's Magazine* 4 (1904).

FIGURE 176. "Pea-Nut Sellers in Savannah." Published in *Harper's Weekly* 14 (1870).

Twice-Told Tales

Although tale-telling was an important leisure-time activity among the slaves, and later the freedmen, relatively few pictures representing that theme have survived, if ever they existed. Perhaps simply watching one person talk to another did not inspire artists to produce something picturesque in the genre tradition. A few of the folktale pictures in our collection represent literary figures made famous by Joel Chandler Harris's stories about Uncle Remus and Br'er Rabbit or by the writings of other postbellum authors (figs. 177–184). To be sure, these images of black folk entertaining white listeners do not relate immediately to the purpose of this study, which, it will be remembered, is to examine how black folk entertained *themselves* in their leisure time. But we know from nineteenth-century sources that the Br'er Rabbit tales originated among black storytellers sitting around their own hearth fires or campfires (figs. 185–187), then moved from the slave cabins to white children in the Big House. Before there was a Joel Chandler Harris, there was a Br'er Rabbit who talked to black children about his animal friends and their adventures. And so the tales were told twice—first, from black storytellers to black listeners, and then from black to white listeners.

Not always was the storyteller a male: in Kemble's "Poor Old Sue Tells Her Story" (fig. 179) an elderly woman holds two white children spellbound with a tale that obviously is fantastic. And not always were the listeners children: "In the Cave" (fig. 177) shows an adolescent caught in the grip of a master tale-teller, and "A Cross-Road Lounger" (fig. 178) shows a young farmer holding forth on a subject that intrigues his white male audience but distresses the two young women; indeed, one of them appears to be shocked.

Richard Brooke's "The 'Coon Hunt" (fig. 187) depicts a group of eight black males seated around a campfire, swapping tales after a long day of hunting. The fire in the lower center of the picture lights up their faces and, despite a disparity in ages—they range from pre-adolescent to elderly—the strong bonding among the men is much in evidence. One of the older men tells his tale with serious mien and expansive gestures, while the others listen intently. But when he has finished, he will be challenged by someone with an even more preposterous tale. And thus this will continue on into the night.

Children Making Music

For American artists in search of subjects for their artworks, the mid-nineteenth century was the era of the child or, more precisely, the era of the boy—depicted by artists at all stages of his growth, from babyhood to adolescence, and under all circumstances, interacting socially with members of his family, playing with his friends, helping with house and farm chores, and generally participating in community life.[16] It was inevitable that some artists would be inspired to produce paintings and drawings of black boys, and, occasionally, black girls.

Although artists generally represent black children as carrying the same social responsibilities as black adults, attending religious meetings and social gatherings with them and working alongside them in the fields, there were some chores specifically associated with children and music-making. As discussed above, the contemporary imagery includes girls using animal horns and the straight bugle as signaling instruments to summon plantation workers to breakfast or to the fields (figs. 142 and 143); boys and girls singing lullabies to

FIGURE 177. Edward Windsor Kemble. "In the Cave." 1884. Pen and ink. Published in *The Adventures of Huckleberry Finn (Tom Sawyer's Comrade)*, by Mark Twain. New York: Charles L. Webster and Company, 1891.

FIGURE 178. Dalziel and Markley. "A Cross-Road Lounger." Mixed media. Published in *America Revisited*, by George Augustus Sala. 3d. ed. London: Vizetelley and Company, 1883.

FIGURE 179. Edward Windsor Kemble. "Poor Old Sue Tells Her Story." Pen and ink. Published in *Daddy Jake the Runaway, and Short Stories Told After Dark by "Uncle Remus,"* by Joel Chandler Harris. New York: Century Company, 1896.

FIGURE 180. Arthur Burdett Frost. "You Wanter Hear a Tale? . . ." Mixed media. Published in *The Tar-Baby and Other Rhymes of Uncle Remus,* by Joel Chandler Harris. New York: D. Appleton and Company, 1904.

FIGURE 181. Edward Windsor Kemble. "The Story-Teller." Pen and ink. Published in "Middle Georgia Rural Life," by Richard M. Johnston. *Century Magazine* 43 (1892).

FIGURE 182. Leigh Richmond Miner. "A Cabin Tale." Photograph. Published in *Joggin' Erlong*, by Paul Laurence Dunbar. New York: Dodd, Mead and Company, 1906.

FIGURE 183. Leigh Richmond Miner. "A Cabin Tale." Photograph. Published in *Joggin' Erlong*.

FIGURE 184. Leigh Richmond Miner. "A Cabin Tale." Photograph. Published in *Joggin' Erlong*.

FIGURE 185. Hampton Institute Camera Club. [Male Story Teller.] Photograph. Published in *Candle Lightin' Time,* by Paul Laurence Dunbar. New York: Dodd, Mead, and Company, 1901.

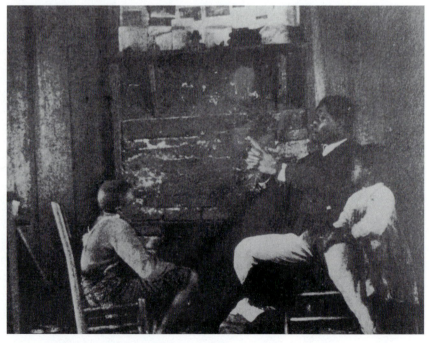

FIGURE 186. Hampton Institute Camera Club. [Male Story Teller.] Photograph. Published in *Candle Lightin' Time. . .* , 122.

FIGURE 187. Richard Norris Brooke. "The 'Coon Hunt—Telling Stories Round the Camp Fire." Wood engraving. Published in *Harper's Weekly* 16 (1872).

their young charges (figs. 150 and 151); and boys as water-carriers at corn-shucking festivals (figs. 155 and 158). Some scenes show boys as independent workers—for example, as a ferryman fiddling during a slack period in the day, in "Jim, the Ferry Boy" (fig. 189), or as a cowherder playing his quills as he drives the cows homeward in "Blowing the Quills" (fig. 195). In all these instances, the child-as-worker improvises music appropriate for the occasion, and most times is given the freedom to play anything he or she chooses, whether appropriate or not.

The black child early learns to recognize city streets as a source of income, and a number of images show him as peddler (fig. 175) and as street musician (fig. 196). Like the adult street crier, the boy invents his own distinctive cries, sometimes in competition with adults. Some of our child-worker images represent actual children, as, for example, the boy pictured in "Spots! Git yuh Fresh Spots" (fig. 175), who plies his trade as a fish-seller on the streets of Hampton, Virginia, and Jim, the ferry boy (fig. 189), a native of Waterview, Virginia, who ferries customers across the Great Kanawha River.

Two young boys in Jacksonville, Florida, depicted in "Professors of 'Chin-Music' " (fig. 196), have worked out a way to call attention to their wares by producing music with their jaws. Artist-correspondent Joseph Becker, who made a sketch of the pair, later engraved for publication, explains the phenomenon:

> The small performer, after collecting his audience of gaping idlers, will open his mouth, at the same time causing the air to pass vocally over the chords of the larynx, and by striking the cheek and maxilliary joint in a peculiar way, will emit a sound half-explosive and half-resonant. The note given by this natural drum is compared, for quality, to the cracking of a filbert under a hammer. At the same time it partakes of a vocal character, and has a perfect gamut of expression, so that a skilled professor can play with ease the popular and patriotic airs of the day. . . . Sometimes two or more performers will travel as a chorus. . . . The young musician generally adds to his choir the "pat-foot" of the plantations.[17]

"Boy" Rhythm Bands

When black boy brass bands became very popular nationwide during the last quarter of the nineteenth century, primarily because of the exposure they received through touring with minstrel shows, street boy musicians took notice and began to organize their own bands. Lacking money to obtain musical training and to purchase instruments, they trained themselves and made their own instruments. Most common were the bottle bands, composed of small boys playing on bottles of various sizes, to which were added one or two melodic instruments and percussion.

The band shown in "Music by the 'Bottle Band'" (fig. 200), which employs five bottles, a mouth organ, and a tambourine, regularly plays "fantastic but harmonious" music at train stops just outside of Charleston, South Carolina, earning "substantial contributions" for its efforts.[18] A bottle band in Florida, "The Jug Band of Palatka, Fla." (fig. 202), is composed of older boys, whose facial expressions indicate they take quite seriously the business of making music; they include three bottle blowers, the requisite mouth-harpist, and a boy beating two sticks together to provide the percussive element.

A "boy band" that plays evenings at a hotel in Fernandina, Florida, "The Juvenile Band" (fig. 201), is composed of quite young boys, of whom five play tin trumpets, two play drums made from boxes, and one plays home-made cymbals. Indeed, all the instruments are homemade. As one guest observed, "If there was not much music in the performance, there was certainly a rhythm in the stroke and a prodigious earnestness in the efforts of the young musicians."[19]

Despite their many duties, African-American boys find time to spend with their friends and to entertain each other, above all with music. Artworks depict them experimenting with producing sounds on the mandolin, a relatively new instrument for black music-makers at that time, in two photographs by John H. Tarbell, "The Nursing-Place of Minstrelsy" (fig. 198) and "My Gal Is a High-Born Lady" (fig. 199). In the first photograph, a boy plays the instrument for his three friends, but it is difficult for the viewer to determine, from the expression on their faces, whether he is successful in impressing them. Nevertheless, he is persistent, despite the snickering of the fellow on his right. On the other hand, the teenage mandolin player in the other photograph (fig. 199) obviously is quite in control of his situation, for the young woman who listens to his song seems to be entranced.

In addition to learning new instruments, boys also enjoy opportunities to show off their skills on old standbys, the banjo and the jew's-harp, as depicted in "Negro Minstrels" (fig. 193) and "The Jew's-Harp" (fig. 197). In the latter picture, one of the boys whittles (making a flute?) as he listens, perhaps with the intention of joining his friend later in playing duets. Finally, there is a charming image of a trio of small singers, two girls and a boy, in "A Few Low, Sweet Chords" (fig. 188), who entertain a white woman reclining on a couch and listening intently. The boy, who seems to be the lead singer, accompanies the singing on his guitar.

Boys also enjoy entertaining themselves, particularly on the fiddle, as in "Jim, the Ferry Boy" (fig. 189) and in "Music Hath Charms" (fig. 190). Despite his abject poverty, the boy in the latter picture (fig. 190) has come to know the power of music to lift him above life's turmoil. He smiles to himself as he pulls a melody from his pathetic, homemade fiddle and taps the beat with his left foot. And there is the young musician in Moser's "The Whistler" (fig. 194), who whistles a lonesome tune, accompanying himself on the banjo as he drifts away into a world of his reveries.

Whistling was a favorite pastime of the ex-slaves, especially among boys and young men. A visitor to Lynchburg, Virginia, noted that in that region the black whistlers organized themselves into gangs according to the plantations where they were born and staged informal evening concerts in Lynchburg. The members of a gang would stand with their backs to a wall, hands in pockets, and whistle the songs of their plantation. "Other gangs pass, whistling their

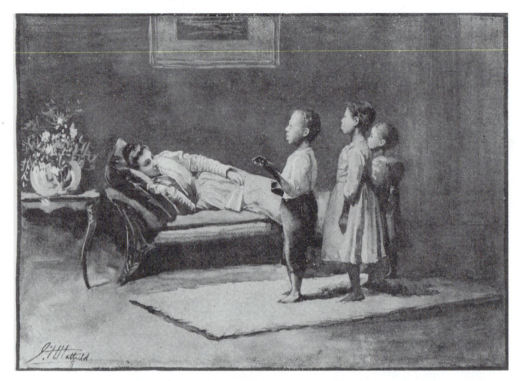

FIGURE 188. Joseph H. Hatfield. "A Few Low, Sweet Chords Vibrated upon the Moonlit Air." Wash. Published in "Tony," by Mary A. P. Stansbury. *New England Magazine* n.s. 8 (1893).

loudest and best, which incites the first [gang] to displays of their fullest capacity; and thus the concert goes on."[20]

Teachers and Pupils

Henry Ossawa Tanner (1859–1937), an African-American artist whose genre paintings brought him wide acclaim, refers to the theme of teaching the young in his two pictures of boys learning how to play the banjo, "Dis Heah's a Fus'-Class Thing . . ." (fig. 191) and "The Banjo Lesson" (fig. 192).[21] This is serious business for the boys, and their intense concentration is communicated to the viewer, as is also the warm, caring concern of the elderly teachers. Neither teachers nor pupils indicate awareness of the fact that in some quarters the banjo is regarded with disdain—nor would they care—but they do know that imaginative music can be produced on the instrument if it is played correctly, and that it is important that children bring high standards to whatever they are learning. Moreover, it is important that teachers possess endless patience.

FIGURE 189. Wade Whipple. "Jim, the Ferry Boy." Wood engraving. Published in "Jim, the Ferry Boy," by Wade Whipple. *Harper's Young People: An Illustrated Weekly* 2 (1881).

FIGURE 190. William Allen Rogers. "Music Hath Charms." Wood engraving. Published in "The Sea Islands," by Samuel Green W. Benjamin. *Harper's New Monthly Magazine* 57 (1878).

FIGURE 191. Henry Ossawa Tanner. "Dis Heah's a Fus'-Class Thing ter Work Off Bad Tempers Wid." c.1893. Engraving. Published in "Uncle Tim's Compromise on Christmas," by Ruth M. Stuart. *Harper's Young People: An Illustrated Weekly* 15 (1893).

FIGURE 192. Henry Ossawa Tanner. "The Banjo Lesson." 1893. Oil on canvas. 49½ × 35¼ in. Hampton University Museum Collection. Hampton, Virginia. Photo credit: Mike Fischer.

FIGURE 193. Peter Sheaf Newell. "Negro Minstrels." 1887. Charcoal. Published in *Harper's Young People: An Illustrated Weekly* 8 (1887).

FIGURE 194. James Henry Moser. "The Whistler." Wood engraving. Published in *Harper's Young People: An Illustrated Weekly* 8 (1887).

FIGURE 195. Edward Windsor Kemble. "Blowing the Quills." Wood engraving by James Tynan. Published in "The Dance in Place Congo," by George W. Cable. *Century Magazine* 31 (1886).

FIGURE 196. Joseph Becker and William Ludlow Sheppard. "Jacksonville, Fla.— Professors of 'Chin-Music' Displaying Their Accomplishments in Front of the Market." Wood engraving. Published in *Frank Leslie's Illustrated Weekly Newspaper* 32 (1871).

FIGURE 197. Clifton H. Johnson. "The Jew's-Harp." Photograph. Published in *Highways and Byways of the South,* by Clifton Johnson. New York: Macmillan Company, 1904.

FIGURE 198. John H. Tarbell. "The Nursing-Place of Minstrelsy." Photograph. Published in "Southern Silhouettes," by Pauline Carrington Bouvre. *New England Magazine* n.s. 43 (1910).

Thomas Eakins's painting "Negro Boy Dancing" (fig. 207) and its study (fig. 206), focus on the same theme as do Tanner's—the importance of applying high standards to the learning experience—except that here an elderly man teaches a young boy how to dance rather than play a musical instrument. The boy has an earnest expression on his face; with eyes fixed in space, he bites his lower lip and strains for all his worth as he tries to execute the step correctly. He is watched closely by his teacher and the young man who accompanies the dancing on his banjo, and there is no doubt he will be warmly praised when he executes the steps correctly.

Figure 199. John H. Tarbell. "My Gal Is a High-Born Lady." Photograph. Published in "The New Generation Down in Dixie." *Frank Leslie's Illustrated Weekly Newspaper* 85 (1897).

FIGURE 200. "On the Observation Platform of a Vestibule Train, Entering Charleston, S.C.—Music by the 'Bottle Band.' " Pen and ink. Published in *Frank Leslie's Illustrated Weekly Newspaper* 68 (1889).

FIGURE 201. Samuel Green Wheeler Benjamin. "The Juvenile Band, Fernandina." Pen and ink. Published in "The Sea Islands," by Samuel Green Wheeler Benjamin. *Harper's New Monthly Magazine* 57 (1878).

FIGURE 202. J. G. Mangold. "The Jug Band of Palatka, Fla." Photograph. Published in *Frank Leslie's Illustrated Weekly Newspaper* 72 (1891).

Boy Street Dancers

Like the diminutive street musicians, small boy dancers learned to use the streets and other public places as sources of income, as shown in Frank Mayer's "Jack Ashore" (fig. 203) and Kemble's "On with the Dance" (fig. 204). Accompaniment is not essential, though it adds a more sophisticated tone to the performance—as when the boy in "A Virginny Breakdown" (fig. 208) accompanies his friend on the jew's harp—nor is the objective solely to make money. Dancers dance for the sheer joy of dancing—for friends or for themselves, as depicted in "Monday Morning" (fig. 209) and "Dancing in the Sun" (fig. 213). They learn the latest steps from each other or from watching adults, and they are not averse to expropriating ideas from their elders, as shown in the "The Cake-Walk" (fig. 205).

J. Wells Champney's "A Jolly Raftful" (fig. 211) depicts an actual event: an extended family floating on a raft down the Mississippi River after a flood has destroyed the family home cheers its members as best it can by encouraging

FIGURE 203. Frank [=Francis] Mayer. "Jack Ashore." Wood engraving. Published in "Old Baltimore and Its Merchants." *Harper's New Monthly Magazine* 40 (1880).

FIGURE 204. Edward Windsor Kemble. "On with the Dance." Watercolor. Published in *American Illustrators,* by Francis Hopkinson Smith. New York: Charles Scribner's Sons, 1892.

FIGURE 205. Edward Windsor Kemble. "The Cake-Walk." Pen and ink. Published in "The Sports of Negro Children," by Timothy Shaler Williams. *St. Nicholas: An Illustrated Magazine for Boys and Girls* 30 (1903).

FIGURE 206. Thomas Eakins. "The Boy." Study for "Negro Boy Dancing." Probably 1877, oil on canvas. .533 × .228 (1 × 9); framed: .616 × .310 × .032 (24¼ × 12³⁄₁₆ × 1¼). Collection of Mr. and Mrs. Paul Mellon, © 1998 Board of Trustees, National Gallery of Art, Washington, D.C.

FIGURE 207. Thomas Eakins. "Negro Boy Dancing." 1878. Watercolor. 18⅛ × 22⅝ in. Metropolitan Museum of Art, Fletcher Fund, 1925 (acc. no. 25.97.1). New York, New York.

FIGURE 208. John Adams Elder. "A Virginny Breakdown." c.1880. Oil on canvas. 18½ × 22¼ in. Virginia Museum of Fine Arts, Richmond. The Virginiana Art Fund. © 1999 Virginia Museum of Fine Arts. Richmond, Virginia. Photograph by Ron Jennings.

the boys to dance, hoping thereby to defer thinking about the family's troubles until a later time.

Another aspect of the "teaching" motif is the theme of learning from one's peers, as in "Ragtime" (fig. 212). The outdoor setting for the dance lesson is the porch of a rather dilapidated cabin, its only furniture a wooden box that serves as a seat for the banjoist. Six boys, ranging in age from about six or eight to the post-adolescent years, expend great energy in trying to execute correctly the dance steps of ragtime, the older ones serving as models for the younger ones. Gone is the heyday of the Pigeon Wing and the Breakdown: those dances are now old-fashioned. Ragtime is the latest fad, and these boys intend to do it properly. The adult who plays the banjo takes no active part in the exercise; his responsibility is to provide accompaniment—obviously in ragtime style—which he supplements with his foot stomping.

Leisure Time: Women and Girls

Relatively rare are images of black women and girls as strong contributors to the expressive culture of African-Americans in the nineteenth century. Primarily, they are shown as companions to men: as busy wives and mothers in family scenes; as shy, teasing adolescents in courtship-rituals scenes; as admiring spectators in crowd scenes; and in supportive roles as dancing partners, particularly when men are taking dashing, extravagant steps that call for the balance offered by daintier female hops and skips. In the fields and in the factories, women work alongside men, and worship alongside them in prayer meetings. To be sure, women sometimes are depicted in leadership roles in religious services or, at least, in attention-getting roles (figs. 113–116), where they may address the congregation as lay leaders or conduct congregational singing.

If artists generally fail to take notice of the strength and beauty of black women, or, if after noticing, fail to transfer those qualities to their palettes, there yet are a few scenes that point up the independent spirit and drive of black women. There are the street peddlers discussed earlier, for example, and the young woman, also discussed, who teaches children to read the Bible on Sunday mornings (fig. 127). Additionally, there are the frisky adolescents in "The Colored Band" (fig. 210), whose irrepressible spirits and "second line" dancing threaten to throw the male band's marching into disarray, and the coquettish young woman using the dance as a way to flirt in "Make a Pretty Motion" (fig. 222).[22] Finally, there is the smiling, well-composed young woman in "Mr. and Mrs. Newlywed's Next 'French' Cook" (fig. 247), who picks at the mandolin cradled in her arms with never a thought for the totally disheveled kitchen, where dirty dishes and kitchen utensils are all about her, on the table, on the floor, on the stove; nor does she give a thought to the dinner that must be prepared for her employer by a certain time.

Two scenes represent mature women—no, actually elderly women—who are shown enjoying themselves in exploring forbidden activities away from the presence of men. In Carol McPherson's photograph of "So I Kept on Jes a Steppin' It Off" (fig. 220), a small elderly woman, her head wrapped in a turban and both hands holding her skirt high in a curtsy position, smiles as she begins to move into a dance forbidden by the church: "De snake dance is a queer kin' er dance dat a ole cunger 'ooman taught me in Ferginny. So I kept on jes a steppin' it off, en' 'fo' I knowed what I wuz doin', I wuz gibbin' 'em de snake dance."[23]

Another picture (fig. 221) shows four women (housewives?), gathered in the spinning room of a cabin, who apparently have stopped work for a morning break. The conversation has led to the subject of dancing, and the oldest member of the group, a white-haired woman, jumps to a clear space in the room to demonstrate her point, "Some kin' er debil dance, whar you stan's on your toes an' spreads your skirts."[24] She lifts her voluminous skirt high as she whirls

FIGURE 209. R. Colburn. "Monday Morning, or the Tender Passion." 1877. Mixed media. Courtesy of the Library of Congress. Washington, D.C.

FIGURE 210. Mrs. K. Colburn [or C. H. Harris?]. "The Colored Band." 1887. Mixed media. Courtesy of the Library of Congress. Washington, D.C.

FIGURE 211. James Wells Champney. "A Jolly Raftful—Taking the Flood Good-Naturedly." Pen and ink. Published in "Swept Away—Down the Mississippi," by Edward S. Ellis. *St. Nicholas: An Illustrated Magazine for Boys and Girls* 10 (1883).

FIGURE 212. J. Campbell Phillips. "Ragtime." Pen and ink. Illustration for *Plantation Sketches*. New York: R. H. Russell, 1899. Print Collection, Miriam and Ira D. Wallach Division of Art, Prints and Photographs, New York Public Library. Astor, Lenox and Tilden Foundations. New York, New York.

FIGURE 213. [Maria]
Howard Weeden.
"Dancing in the Sun."
Wash (?). Published in
Songs of the Old South,
by Howard Weeden.
New York: Doubleday,
Page, and Company, 1900.

about, explaining the dance steps as she moves, while the other three women sing an accompaniment for her, two of them also marking the beat with their hand-clapping.

Then there is the scene (fig. 210), cited previously, which features adolescent girls, who generally are given short shrift by nineteenth-century artists, being restricted to admiring the male figure, often from a distance, and applauding his intricate dance steps or weird banjo harmonies. In "The Colored Band" (fig. 210), five or more girls weave in and out of the line-of-march of a band on parade, to the great consternation of some of the young servicemen and the drum major. The girls, very composed, seem intent on demonstrating that they, too, know the latest dance steps, and as "second liners" of the parade, they intend to execute them.

Leisure Time: Rural and Urban

Artists, artist-reporters, writers, journalists, travelers—all speculated about how the ex-slaves would spend their leisure time at the end of the workday, or the workweek, now that they were their own masters and no longer obligated to respond to the call of overseer or slaveholder. Not surprisingly, music and the dance provide answers to the questions: in impromptu performances, dancers vie with each other in executing the older plantation-type dances—e.g., the Pigeon Wing and the Breakdown—or more faddish dances before appreciative individuals or groups of critical but admiring spectators (figs. 214–222). Group dances retain their popularity for the black community, particularly Saturday-night dances and celebrations relating to Christmas (figs. 223–228), and a few activities take the ex-slaves away from their rural homes into the cities, where they mingle with whites and other blacks on the streets to celebrate events of mutual interest, such as the New Orleans Carnival or voter registration (figs. 229–230 and 232).

FIGURE 214. Howard Helmick. "Uncle Henson Cuts the Pigeon Wing." Pen and ink. Published in *The Story of My Life*, by Mary A. Livermore. Hartford, Connecticut: A. D. Worthington and Company, 1897.

Like the dancers, talented ex-slave musicians entertain their fellows with endless improvised songs, in which they sing of past events, personal histories, current history, politics—anything that their listeners want to be reminded of, or to learn. As in the antebellum years, fiddles and banjos remain the favored instruments for accompanying singing (figs. 233–246), but the new-on-the-scene guitars and mandolins do attract the attention of some music-makers (figs. 247 and 251–252).

Community Dance Bands

The Saturday-night dance, a plantation custom of long standing, increased in popularity after Emancipation, as did also the tradition for relying on the fiddle to provide the music, accompanied often by only a patter. Two scenes, "Saturday Evening's Dance" (fig. 223) and "Terpsichore in the Flat Creek Quarters" (fig. 224), show dancers in action, the latter kept in order by the stentorian tones of the dance master, who calls the sets for cotillions and quadrilles. But at least one dance scene, "Some One Produced a Fiddle" (fig. 217), includes no instruments at all, at least, none are in view, and not even a patter is present to provide rhythmic sounds. In the dance pictures there are references to conventional motifs that point up the importance of the musicians: the fiddler (or

FIGURE 215. William Allen Rogers. "Quorum Dances a Break-Down." Mixed media. Published in "Canoe-mates: A Story of the Everglades," by Kirk Munroe. *Harper's Young People: An Illustrated Weekly* 13 (1892).

FIGURE 216. Edward Windsor Kemble. "In the Store." Crayon. Published in "Sugar-Making in Louisiana," by Eugene V. Smalley. *Century Magazine* 35 (1887).

FIGURE 217. Willard Poinsette Snyder. "Some One Produced a Fiddle, and They Danced." Pen and ink. Published in "Wakulla," by Kirk Munroe. *Harper's Young People: An Illustrated Weekly* 6 (1884).

FIGURE 218. "Lucindy." Pen and ink. Published in "Lucindy," by Ruth M. Stuart. *Harper's New Monthly Magazine* 84 (1892).

FIGURE 219. William Ludlow Sheppard. "Ol' Lijah Wuz de Bes' Man; He'd Cut de Pigin-Wing." Pen and ink. Published in "Ol' Virginny Reel." *Weh Down Souf and Other Poems,* by Daniel Webster Davis. Cleveland: Helman-Taylor Company, 1897.

FIGURE 220. Carol McPherson. "So I Kept on Jes a Steppin' It Off." Photograph. Published in *In Old Alabama. Being the Chronicles of Miss Mouse, the Little Black Merchant,* by Anne Hobson. New York: Doubleday, Page and Company, 1903.

FIGURE 221. John Wolcott Adams. "Some Kin' er Debil Dance." Mixed media. Published in "Ole Marse and Aunt Nancy," by Virginia Frazer Boyle. *Harper's Weekly* 53 (1909).

FIGURE 222.   J. W. Otto. "Make a Pretty Motion." Photograph. Published in *Planta-tion Songs for My Lady's Banjo* . . . , by Eli Sheppherd. New York: R. H. Russell, 1901.

FIGURE 223. Alfred R. Waud. "Saturday Evening's Dance." Wood engraving. Published in "Scenes on a Cotton Plantation." *Harper's Weekly* 11 (1867).

FIGURE 224. "Terpsichore in the Flat Creek Quarters." Mixed media. Published in *Scribner's Monthly* 21 (1881).

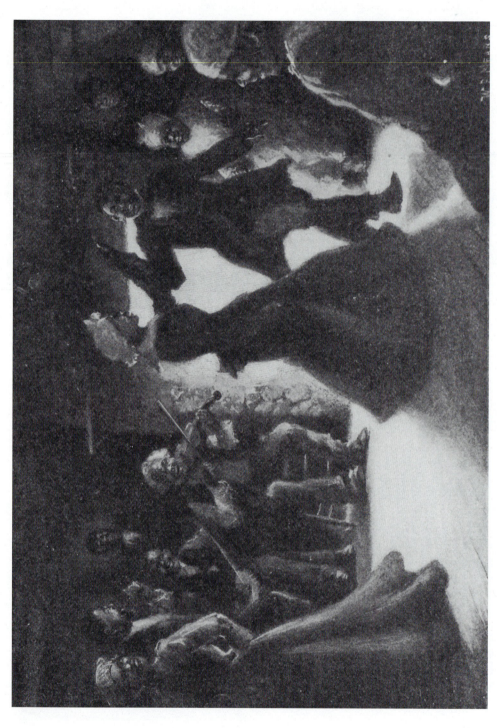

Figure 225. W. E. Mears. "Celebrating Christmas." Mixed media. Published in "Chris'mus," by H. H. Mears. *Harper's Weekly* 55 (1911).

FIGURE 226. William Ludlow Sheppard. "Holiday Games at Richmond, Va.—'The Cake Walk.'" Wood engraving. Published in *Frank Leslie's Illustrated Weekly Newspaper* 31 (1870).

FIGURE 227. "Walking for the Cake." Pen and ink. Published in "The Coloured People in the United States: In the South," by T. L. Robinson. *Leisure Hour* 38 (1889).

FIGURE 228. Edward Windsor Kemble. "De John Connahs Comin'." 1891. Pen and ink. Published in "Christmas at Buchoi, a North Carolina Rice Plantation," by Rebecca Cameron. *Ladies Home Journal* (1891).

FIGURE 229. William Ludlow Sheppard and James Wells Champney. "The Carnival—White and Black Join in Its Masquerading." Wood engraving by F. Juengling. Published in *The Great South,* by Edward King. Hartford, Connecticut: American Publishing Company, 1875.

FIGURE 230. Solomon Eytinge. "De Jubilee Am Come—Fourth of July, 1876." Wood engraving. Published in *Harper's Weekly* 20 (1876).

FIGURE 231. Joseph Becker and John N. Hyde. "Pennsylvania—Scene in the Schuylkill County Prison at Pottsville—The 'Prisoners' March' for Exercise in the Corridor." Wood engraving. Published in "A Noted Pennsylvania Prison." *Frank Leslie's Illustrated Weekly Newspaper* 56 (1883).

FIGURE 232. Alfred Wordsworth Thompson. "Registration at the South—Scene at Asheville, North Carolina." Wood engraving by John C. Karst. Published in *Harper's Weekly* 11 (1867).

FIGURE 233. James D. Smillie. "Black Joe, the Fiddler." Pen and ink. Published in "Phil's Fairies," by Mrs. W. F. Hays. *Harper's Young People: An Illustrated Magazine* 2 (1881).

FIGURE 234. William Henry Huddle. "Old Slave." c.1889. Oil on canvas. 35½ × 27½ in. Dallas Museum of Art, The Karl and Esther Hoblitzelle Collection, gift of the Hoblitzelle Foundation. Dallas, Texas.

FIGURE 235. Hampton Institute Camera Club. "Step wid de Banjo an' Glide wid de Fiddle." Photograph. Published in *Speakin' o' Christmas*, by Paul Laurence Dunbar. New York: Dodd, Mead, and Company, 1904.

FIGURE 236. William Ludlow Sheppard. "Negro Life in the South." Wood engraving. Published in *Harper's Weekly* 16 (1872).

FIGURE 237. Alfred Wordsworth Thompson. "Scene on a Southern Plantation." Wood engraving. Published in *Harper's Weekly* 12 (1868).

FIGURE 238. J. W. Otto. "Plantation Song." Photograph. Published in *Plantation Songs for My Lady's Banjo . . .* , by Eli Sheppherd. New York: R. H. Russell, 1901.

FIGURE 239. Thomas Eakins. "The Banjo Player." Study for "Negro Boy Dancing." Probably 1877. Oil on canvas mounted on cardboard, .495 × .379 (19½ × 14⅞); framed: .579 × .457 × .035 (22¹³⁄₁₆ × 18 × 1⅜). Collection of Mr. and Mrs. Paul Mellon, © 1998 Board of Trustees, National Gallery of Art, Washington, D.C.

FIGURE 240. William Ludlow Sheppard. "An Artist Selecting an Instrument." Wood engraving. Published in *Frank Leslie's Illustrated Weekly Newspaper* 32 (1871).

FIGURE 241. Hampton Institute Camera Club. "Chris'mus Is A-Comin'." Photograph. Published in *Poems of Cabin and Field*, by Paul Laurence Dunbar. New York: Dodd, Mead, and Company, 1899.

FIGURE 242. John P. Pemberton. "Jerry's Melodious Bass Broke into the Old Song." Crayon. Published in "Jerry," by Ruth M. Harrison. *Putnam's Monthly 7* (1909).

caller) typically wears more formal attire than the dancers (including a top hat and long frock coat), usually is placed in the foreground to the right or left of the dancers, and generally has a commanding air. A visitor who remembered the Saturday-night dances of slavery time noticed that the ex-slaves took up the new ballroom dance, the cotillion, and commented: "With the cotillion a new and very important office, that of 'caller-out' has become a necessity. The 'caller-out,' though of no less importance than the fiddler, is second to none other. He not only calls out the figures, but explains them at length to the igno-rant, sometimes accompanying them through the performance. He is never at a loss, 'Gemmen to de right!' being a sufficient refuge in case of embarrass-ment, since this always calls forth a full display of the dancers' agility and gives much time."[25]

Store-Bought and Homemade Instruments

Throughout the slavery era the fiddle and the banjo proved very useful to black folk. In view of this, it is not surprising that these instruments retained their popularity into the twentieth century, except that by the end of the nine-teenth century the novelty of the guitar threatened to turn it into a rival of the banjo. Almost anyone could play the banjo, but not anyone could become a master banjoist. In "An Artist Selecting an Instrument" (fig. 240), William Sheppard depicts how the good banjoist chooses his instrument carefully, hov-ered over by an experienced salesman, who is anxious to please a top client. The salesman knows that the boy who is watching the transaction has the potential to become a future customer.

Several images demonstrate the versatility of the banjo: it is shown quietly accompanying young male singers surrounded by their friends and admirers (figs. 245 and 246); offering a decisive, upbeat strumming for a hand-clapping, foot-stomping comrade (fig. 243); giving solicitous support to a modest young dancer (figs. 207 and 239); and adding its raucous voice to the songs of friends on a Saturday night (fig. 244). Whether in high spirits or pensive mood, the master finds his banjo ready to respond to abrupt shifts or subtle changes in mood.

During the slave-trade period, the best fiddlers and banjoists somehow managed to obtain store-bought instruments, whether purchased for them by their masters or with money they had saved from meager earnings, and it is probable that those who played flutes, straight trumpets, tambourines, and tri-angles also owned their instruments. The question of cello ownership, how-ever, presents an enigma. A large, expensive instrument, the cello would hardly have been priced low enough to enable an ex-slave to purchase it, even over a lifetime of savings.

FIGURE 243. J. W. Otto. "Den I Reckon de Wise Folks Might an' May . . ." Photograph. Published in *Plantation Songs for My Lady's Banjo, and Other Negro Lyrics and Monologues,* by Eli Sheppherd. New York: R. H. Russell, 1901.

FIGURE 244. William Ludlow Sheppard. "Echoes of Old Plantation Melodies." Wood engraving by R. Staudenbaur. Published in *Harper's Weekly* 28 (1884).

The scenes in this collection that show the cello as a member of a dance ensemble represent formal dances where the cello fits beautifully in the scheme for the evening (compare antebellum figs. 51–52 with postbellum figs. 134–135 and 254). To be sure, on other occasions the cello is called upon to accompany a Pigeon Wing dancer (fig. 216) and to help to advertise a Cake Walk (fig. 249). Is the cello a status instrument or simply an overgrown fiddle? What was its role in the dance ensemble? Did wealthy white men purchase the instrument for their black protégés in the same way as they purchased fiddles? Did the instrument belong to the plantation community rather than to an individual? Was the cello borrowed for the special occasion? No answers to these questions are forthcoming at this time.

When black music-makers could not purchase instruments they constructed them from whatever materials were at hand. In a letter to the editor of the *New York Sun* in 1894, an anonymous contributor observed: "Most plantations had a bugler who owned an old wooden bugle five or six feet long. These bugles were made generally of poplar wood coated with tar and kept under water for several days. Soaking it kept the instrument from shrinking, and gave it a resonant sound. The bugle's primary purpose was to serve as a signal

FIGURE 245. Frank Buchser. "The Song of Mary Blaine." 1870–71. Oil on canvas. Gottfried Keller Collection. Solothurn Art Museum. Solothurn, Switzerland.

FIGURE 246. John Whetten Ehninger. "Music Hath Charms." Wood engraving. Published in the *Illustrated Christian Weekly* 3 (1873).

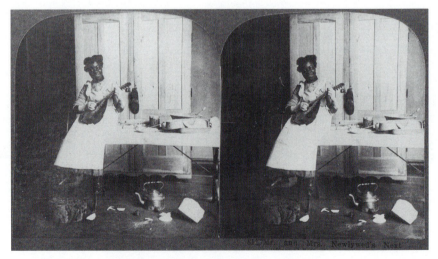

FIGURE 247. "Mr. and Mrs. Newlywed's Next 'French' Cook." Late 19th century. Stereograph. New York City. Photographs and Prints Division. Schomburg Center for Research in Black Culture, New York Public Library, Astor, Lenox and Tilden Foundations. New York, New York.

instrument, but it also served musical purposes, particularly at corn-shucking and other community festivals" (figs. 162 and 163).[26]

There were almost as many ways to make a banjo as there were banjoists. Maurice Thompson, in a letter to the editor of the *Critic*, was impressed by one instrument "the body of which was a flat gourd. . . . which had been flattened by confining it, during its growth, between two boards, and its neck or handle had been cut off and a wooden one with screws attached. . . ."[27] Ex-slave Isaac D. Williams, who made his fiddle from a gourd and used horse hair for the strings and bow, observes that if plenty of rosin is used on the strings, the sound will compare favorably to that of an ordinary violin.[28] Another popular homemade instrument was the quills (fig. 195), made by assembling from three to seven reeds of different sizes and lengths and played by shifting the quills across the lips, thereby producing some "weird" music, according to a few listeners.

Animal parts served as sources for many instruments, particularly horns of various types and bones. Indeed, the bones were polished and admitted to a place of respect in the plantation dance ensemble; no group was considered complete without a pair, or two pairs, of bones dominating the percussion (see also pp. 82–85, 192, and 195).

Special Traditions

Christmas of course brought its own special kinds of joyous activities, particularly the small parties in cabins where the guests gathered to dance to the music of fiddle and banjo, as in "Celebrating Christmas" (fig. 225). Some of the leisure-time activities of the freedmen had no parallels among whites—for example, the Cake Walk, which is shown in "Holiday Games at Richmond, Va.—'The Cakewalk' " (fig. 226) and "Walking for the Cake" (fig. 227). Reports on that event come primarily from states on the southeastern seaboard, where one reporter describes it as a "fete peculiar to the colored race" especially associated with the celebration of Christmas.[29] Though the rites differ from place to place, the Cake Walk essentially is a promenade dance competition, with heavy comic overtones, that allows the contestants to demonstrate certain kinds of parade skills, and the winner to take home the cake. "Walking for the cake" can be quite a formal affair, with contestants and spectators dressed in their finest attire and music provided by a three-piece band (fig. 227). A Cake Walk for church members, who are not permitted to sing worldly music, will allow them to substitute a hymn sung to a vigorous marching tune and to beat the time by clapping their hands.[30] Not surprisingly, black children also have their own Cake Walks (fig. 205).

Closely associated with the Christmas holidays in some places is the John Canoe (also known as Connah, Kuner, Koonering, Kunnering) festival, a procession of sorts that decks most of its marchers in costumes.[31] Kemble's drawing, entitled "De John Connahs Comin' " (fig. 228), represents a procession on a plantation in North Carolina. It is noteworthy that in the several descriptions of the John Canoe festival that have survived in nineteenth-century literature, the costumes and general procedures of John Canoe are similar, whether in the Carolinas, Georgia, or Florida—unlike the Cake Walk, which varies from place to place. Edward Warren, a world traveler who saw a close similarity between the African-American John Kunnering and the performance of Byram in Egypt, describes his first-time experience in watching the procession: "The leading character is the 'ragman,' whose get-up consists in a costume of rags, so arranged that one end of each hangs loose and dangles; two great ox-horns, attached to the skin of a raccoon, which is drawn over the head and the face, leaving apertures only for the eyes and mouth; sandals of the skin of some wild "varmint"; several cow or sheep bells or strings of dried goats' horns hanging about their shoulders, and so arranged as to jingle at every movement; and a short stick of seasoned wood, carried in his hands."[32]

This part of the procession is accompanied by men "arrayed fantastically in ribbons, rags, and feathers," who play all kinds of musical instruments, including one especially associated with the John Canoe festival, the "gumba box," which is made of a wooden frame over which is stretched a tanned sheepskin. After much wild dancing and singing, the other men drop out, leaving the two leaders to compete in exhibiting their best steps and movements, while the singing continues throughout. After the performance, the participants, holding hats in their hands, go from one visitor to another to "gather the harvest of pennies with which every one is provided."[33]

Outdoor City Events

"The Carnival" (fig. 229) shows crowds of masked revelers filling the city streets of New Orleans, where, according to the picture's caption, "White and Black Join in Its Masquerading" (probably in reference to Mardi Gras). The viewer's attention immediately is drawn to a black family in the lower-right foreground, whose members dance to the music of a banjo played by the father. The artist has painted them in sharper detail than any other group except for a trio of whites in the front-center foreground. "Registration at the South" (fig. 232), which records an actual event, is of historic significance for its pictorial documentation of the first time ex-slaves have been able to register to vote, this made possible under the provisions of the Reconstruction Act and its supplements. The crowds milling about in Asheville, North Carolina, appreciate the gravity of the occasion, particularly the ex-slaves, of whom two turn to the dance, possibly as a way of relieving their anxiety and expressing their incredulity that this thing has actually come to pass, that blacks truly can register to vote.

Instrumental Street Music

Novel combinations of instruments are shown in some of the street-music scenes; for example, "In the Store" (fig. 216) depicts a man dancing the Pigeon Wing, accompanied by cello and accordion; "I'se Ringin' fo' de Cake-Walk" (fig. 249), shows a trio of music-makers outside the entrance to a fair grounds, where they combine the sounds of a cello (?) and banjo with that of a huge bell ringing continuously; and a photograph of two young men leaning against the outside window of a boarded-up house (fig. 252) pairs a guitarist and a mandolinist.

Perhaps one of the most original sounds is that concocted by the young musician in "The Cheery Minstrel" (fig. 248), who specializes in "train" music—that is, he travels on trains from car to car, playing his music as he moves along. Writer Edward King, who made a sketch which he later engraved and published, observes: "The cheery minstrel, whose portrait our artist has given, makes music on the cars between St. Louis and the State capital [Jefferson City, Missouri]. He is one of the celebrities of Missouri, known to thousands of the traveling public, and when the Legislature is in session, and the tide of travel is strong, coins many an honest penny, the fruit of much manipulation

FIGURE 248. James Wells Champney. "The Cheery Minstrel." Wood engraving? Published in *The Great South,* by Edward Smith King. Hartford, Connecticut: American Publishing Company, 1875.

"I'se Ringin' fo' de Cake-Walk."

FIGURE 249. William Allen Rogers. "I'se Ringin' fo' de Cake-Walk." Pen and ink. Published in "Scenes on the Midway—Cotton States and International Expositions, Atlanta, Georgia." Published in *Harper's Weekly* 39 (1895).

FIGURE 250. Cassius Marcellus Coolidge. "Street Music." Wood engraving. Published in *Harper's Weekly* (Supplement) 16 (1872).

FIGURE 251. Frank Buchser. "Guitar Player." 1867. Oil on canvas [location unknown].

of harmonicon and triangle."[34] The picture shows him playing the harmonicon and triangle simultaneously, holding the harmonicon to his mouth with his left hand, along with a string to which is attached the triangle, and beating the triangle with his right hand.

Parades of a Sort

"De Jubilee Am Come—Fourth of July, 1876" (fig. 230) represents a parade of black veterans of the Civil War. A march through the countryside, accompanied by stirring music, brings out all the country folk, some of whom join informally in the procession. Little boys, especially, exult at the opportunity to prance along as "second liners." A procession of a different kind is shown in "Pennsylvania—Scene in the Schuylkill County Prison at Pottsville" (fig. 231), of which the subcaption reads "The 'Prisoners' March' for Exercise in the Corridor." Leading the double-file marchers are two black men, who sing vigorously, accompanying themselves on banjos, and are joined by some of the other prisoners, black and white. The scene is reminiscent of the images of antebellum slave coffles, except that the slave trader and his whip are no longer included.

Itinerant Musicians and Vendors of Street Music

A novelty in the history of black dance music is the appearance of the street-music ensemble, which might consist of as few as two performers or as many as five or six (figs. 249–250, 252–255). Frankly commercial in its attitude toward making music, the ensemble can be found in the cities performing on street corners, in barrooms and other public places, and at elite resorts, as well as in rural areas playing for dances in the black community. In several respects, these scenes offer a look into the future, when the various traditions of nineteenth-century African-American music and dance will have merged, along with other musical genres and styles, to produce the new music called jazz (figs. 257–260).

As pointed out above, street-music groups vary in number of players, from very few to as many as a half-dozen or more. Perhaps the most frequently seen and heard is the banjo-fiddle team, as in "Street Music" (fig. 250), which plays on street corners, wharves, and other such public places. The itinerant musicians pictured in "Life Sketches in the Metropolis" (fig. 256) consists of a fiddler, banjoist, player on the bones, and tambourinist. A journalist identifies these performers in the title of his article as "Wandering African Minstrels Performing at a Noted Place of Resort on Harlem Lane," and he gives the instrumentation as fiddle, banjo, flute, and harp. Either the men doubled on instruments, or the artist sketched the group at a different time than the

FIGURE 252. [Mandolin and Guitar Players.] Photograph/stereograph. 1902. Courtesy of the Library of Congress. Washington, D.C.

FIGURE 253. Howard Helmick. "Cotching the Tune." Pen and ink. Published in *The Story of My Life*, by Mary A. Livermore. Hartford, Connecticut: A. D. Worthington and Company, 1897.

FIGURE 254. Arthur Burdett Frost. "The Music for the Dance." Wash. Published in *Harper's Weekly* 35 (1891).

FIGURE 255. Arthur Burdett Frost. "There's Music in the Air." Wood engraving. Published in "The City of Atlanta," by Ernest Ingersoll. *Harper's New Monthly Magazine* 60 (1879).

FIGURE 256. John N. Hyde. "Life Sketches in the Metropolis—Wandering African Minstrels Performing at a Noted Place of Resort on Harlem Lane." Wood engraving. Published in *Frank Leslie's Illustrated Weekly Magazine* 34 (1872).

journalist saw it. We are informed that these "wandering minstrels" are well traveled, having staged their makeshift performances in the leading barrooms on the eastern seaboard and as far west as St. Louis and New Orleans.[35] Judging from the antics of two of the players, their presentations include more than simply making music: undoubtedly, they throw in jokes, perhaps also a dance or two, and exchange much banter among the four of them. Basically, the group is the traditional plantation ensemble, which has discarded its field-hand attire for something a bit more formal and has taken to the streets.

A nocturnal scene, "There's Music in the Air" (fig. 255), shows also a motley group of music-makers—this time gathered in front of a barroom in Atlanta, Georgia—whose purpose is to entertain only themselves. If the three or four spectators in the scene also enjoy the music, that is fine but not essential. As in the "Wandering African Minstrels" (fig. 256), the instruments are the old plantation standbys that have been moved to the city: a banjo and two violins, joined by an accordion and a small straight trumpet. Three men sing loudly, and one man, positioned at the far left of the picture, dances with wild abandon—in fact, to such an extent that he attracts the attention of some of the spectators and musicians. As a group the string players are seemingly oblivious to their surroundings: with heads bent deeply over their instruments, lips closed tightly, and eyes closed or looking into space, they appear to be playing in a different world than that of their companions.

The string band grew increasingly popular among black folk musicians as the nineteenth century drew to a close, and it paved the way for the development of the ragtime and jazz string bands of the early twentieth century. Typical ensembles of the period are shown in Helmick's "Cotching the Tune" (fig. 253) and Frost's "The Music for the Dance" (fig. 254). In the former, a trio of fiddlers stands in the rain under a window, trying to "catch" the melody of the music that pours out the window, and in the Frost scene, the classical post-bellum plantation quartet—two violinists, banjoist, and celloist—is depicted walking across a snow-covered field at night, either on its way to play for an evening dance or returning from such an engagement. By the 1880s, if not earlier, the cello had become a member of the traditional plantation dance orchestra, at least for formal dances, if not on a regular basis.

As for the sound of the music, that remains an enigma. In "Music for the Dance," for example, it can be assumed that at least one fiddle would play the melody; that the banjo would play chordal harmonies; and the cello, a bass line. But what part would the second fiddle play? Indeed, what is the musical role for the second fiddle generally in the black rural dance band? Did the instrument play an obligato above the melody line? The concept of a soprano–alto duo is foreign to plantation-music style, and the contemporary writings of white reporters do not give much attention to the matter, except for a few complaints about the harsh sounds of black fiddlers "scrapping" away on their fiddles. Is it possible that both fiddles played the tune, but improvised as they played, thereby enriching the musical texture, with concessions made for discords? Possibly.

The guitar likewise gained in popularity among African Americans, particularly in the rural South (figs. 251–252). By the end of the nineteenth century it was being used increasingly by a number of itinerant street musicians who sang or played a variety of music, ranging from ballads, hymns, patriotic songs, rag songs, and spirituals, to a newly evolving genre soon to be known throughout America as the blues. It had also begun to take its place alongside the banjo, fiddle, and mandolin as a prominent member of the string bands and jug bands that supplied accompaniment for postbellum dances. Perhaps Swiss painter Frank Buchser, who lived in the United States from 1864 to 1871, has captured in his oil painting, "The Guitar Player" (fig. 251, 1867), one of the earliest pictorial records of a prototype of the early black blues-guitar man.

Avant-garde Painters and Jazz

Up to the present, jazz historians have ignored the extraordinary contributions of the early avant-garde painters to jazz iconography, though these historians have combed the literature for references to the origin of this new music, its performance practice, repertory, and so on. Based on our research findings, we can state with certainty that jazz iconography dates from 1913, the year avant-garde European painters flooded New York City, having come to exhibit their works at the Armory Show (February 15–March 15), and they remained to explore the fascinations of the city. Among them was Francis Picabia, who was taken to a restaurant by friends soon after his arrival in New York, where "for the first time in his life he heard and saw an American Negro sing a 'Coon Song' in characteristic manner. The next day he put upon canvas his impression, making two pictures, each of which he named 'Negro Song' ['Chanson nègre I' and 'Chanson nègre II,' both in 1913]."[36]

Albert Gleizes, another painter smitten with the exotic sounds of jazz, painted "Composition (for 'Jazz')" and "Jazz" (both 1915). Since these artists were cubists, it is somewhat difficult, though not impossible, for the viewer to perceive immediately that the intentions of the artists are to represent jazz in their paintings of swirling lines that interlock with rectangular shapes and sweeping curves.

American painter Charles Demuth, in Europe during the years 1912 to 1914, missed the Armory Show, but after returning to the United States he developed a great enthusiasm for the new music called jazz, influenced by his visits to African-American cabarets. Frequenting clubs in the section of the New York City called "black Bohemia," Demuth and his friends became particularly fond of Barron Wilkin's Little Savoy on West 35th Street and the Marshall Hotel's restaurant on West 53rd Street. Later, both clubs moved to Harlem.

Four of the Demuth jazz paintings in our collection use Marshall's café as the setting, where crepe-paper festoons hang from the low ceiling, and the patrons, with one exception, sit crowded together at café tables pushed to the right background of the scenes, permitting the musicians to occupy most of the foreground of the pictures. The exception, "Cabaret" (Fig. 260), shows the musicians shunted to the upper right background, where they perform on a raised platform above the heads of the patrons, who crowd the remainder of the scene. On this painting, at the bottom right-of-center, Demuth identifies the place as "Barron Wilkin's Little Savoy."

The jazz band consists of four musicians: the banjoist, who has a choice of the instruments he will play, for a second one lies at his feet; the pianist, who plays on an upright piano; a girl singer, who dances in three of the scenes; and the drummer, whose drum set includes the snare drum, bass drum, "top" cymbals, and other percussion. In "Marshall's" (fig. 257) the drummer is mostly cut off the scene on the lower right edge, with only his right hand in view. It is worthy of note that as early as 1916 the drummer has a full drumset, though at that time jazz supposedly was in its infancy as a musical genre. We know the sound of the music being performed, for on the music rack before the pianist is a score of the popular song "Bill Bailey, Won't You Please Come Home?" (dating from 1902).

Although it might appear at first glance that each of the Demuth scenes is different, with closer observation it becomes apparent that "Negro Jazz Band," also known as "Negro Girl Dancer" (fig. 258), and "Negro Jazz Band" (fig. 259) essentially are the same: the artist has simply positioned the musicians differently on the picture and particularized their heads and facial features to suggest a different occasion. Or, perhaps Demuth used the "band" picture (fig. 259) as a study for the more carefully finished "dancer" image (fig. 258).

In his jazz paintings, Demuth has evoked the spirit of the night-life world of New York City's African-American community in the early twentieth century and, in the process, has given us a prototype for the jazz trio or quartet, which would become one of the most popular formats for jazz ensembles in the future.

In conclusion, the collection of artworks we present in this book brings together for the first time a large body of imagery devoted solely to African-American traditional culture of the nineteenth and early twentieth centuries. These visual materials offer researchers an important, but often overlooked, source for investigating and reconstructing the historical foundations of black American slave culture, upon which so much of African-American culture in the United States was based in the twentieth century. The insights gained from study of these works help us to define African-American culture, to identify its themes, and to celebrate its richness as well as its diversity.

The notes for this chapter begin on page 271.

FIGURE 257. Charles Demuth. "Marshall's." 1915. Mixed media on paper. 13 × 8 in. Private collection. Photograph courtesy of Kennedy Galleries, Inc. New York, New York.

FIGURE 258. Charles Demuth. "Negro Jazz Band," also known as "Negro Girl Dancer." 1916. Watercolor and pen. 12⅞ × 7⅞ in. Irwin Goldstein Collection. Photograph courtesy Kurt Muller.

FIGURE 259. Charles Demuth. "Negro Jazz Band." 1916. Watercolor and pen. 13 × 7⅞ in. Irwin Goldstein Collection. Photograph courtesy Kurt Muller.

FIGURE 260. Charles Demuth. "Cabaret: At Barron Wilkin's Little Savoy." 1919. Watercolor and pencil. 8 × 10¼ in. Private collection.

Notes

1. Barrett, "Negro Folk Songs," 238–45.
2. Ibid., 242.
3. "Life and Travel," 491.
4. See, for example, pictures of husking bees in Hills, *Painter's America,* 26, 32, 97.
5. "Corn Shuckin' down South," 4.
6. Barrow, "Georgia Corn-Shucking," 875.
7. Ibid., 875.
8. Ibid., 878.
9. "Virginia Tobacco Mart," 345.
10. "Scenes at the South," 29.
11. "Song of the Oystermen," 122.
12. Cooley, "Mississippi Roustabout," 299.
13. Ibid.
14. Shanley, "Street Cries," 200.
15. Scharf, *History,* 2: 930; Leiding, *Street Cries,* 5.
16. See Hills, *Painter's America,* 74–75, regarding artists' great interest in using white children as subjects for their artworks in the post–Civil War period.
17. "Professors of 'Chin Music,' " 347.
18. "On the Observation Platform," 27.
19. Benjamin, "The Sea Islands," 847.
20. Patten, "Scenes," 2: 541.
21. From all evidence, one of these Tanner artworks (fig. 191) has escaped the attention of Tanner art scholars up to the present. See *Henry Ossawa Tanner,* edited by Dewey F. Mosby et al. (New York: Rizzoli, 1991). The location of the original oil is not known, but our research has confirmed its existence as a magazine illustration in two sources: (1) under the title "Uncle Tim's Compromise on Christmas" in *Harper's Young People* (December 1893), 84; and (2) as "Dis Heah's a Fus-Class Thing ter Work Off Bad Tempers Wid" in *Solomon Crow's Christmas Pockets and Other Tales* by Ruth McEnery Stuart (New York: Harper & Brothers, 1897), frontispiece.
22. The term "second lining" refers to the children who prance on the sidelines during a brass-band parade.
23. Hobson, *In Old Alabama,* frontispiece.
24. Boyle, "Ole Marse," 22.
25. Barrow, "Georgia Corn Shucking," 878.
26. "Corn Shuckin'," 4.
27. Thompson, "Plantation Music," 20.
28. Williams, *Sunshine and Shadow,* 62.
29. "Cake Walk," 261.
30. Bassett, "Going to House Keeping," 208.
31. Several European explorers report on the exploits of the original John Canoe, an African ruler who flourished in the eighteenth century on the coast of Guinea and became a hero to his people for his courage in resisting white traders. See, for example, *A Voyage to Guinea . . . ,* by William Smith (London: Printed for John Nourse, 1744), 116–17; *A Voyage to Guinea, Brasil, and the West Indies . . . ,* by John Atkins (London: Printed for Ward and Chandler, 1737), 75–77. The ex-slave Linda Brent includes a detailed description of a John Canoe festival in *Incidents in the Life of a Slave Girl* (Boston: Published for the Author, 1861).

32. Warren, *Doctor's Experience,* 201–02.

33. Cameron, "Christmas at Buchoi," 6.

34. King, *Great South,* 255.

35. "Wandering Minstrels," 60.

36. "Mr. Picabia Paints 'Coon Songs,' " *New York Herald* (March 18, 1913), 12.

Selected Bibliography

This bibliography is limited to titles cited in the text. For an extensive listing of primary sources that inform about African-American traditional culture, beginning with the colonial period and extending to the threshold of the Harlem Renaissance in the 1920s, see Southern and Wright, *African-American Traditions . . .* (1990).

Aimwell, Absalom (pseud. for Andrew Adgate). *A Pinkster Ode for the Year 1803. Most Respectfully Dedicated to Carolus Africanus, Rex: Thus Rendered in English; King Charles, Captain General and Commander in Chief of the Pinkster Boys.* Albany, New York: Printed Solely for the Purchasers and Others, 1803.

Allen, Richard. *The Life Experience and Gospel Labors of the Rt. Rev. Richard Allen. To Which Is Annexed the Rise and Progress of the African Methodist Episcopal Church in the United States of America. . . .* Philadelphia: Martin and Boden, 1833.

Allen, William, and T. R. H. Thomson. *A Narrative of the Expedition Sent by Her Majesty's Government to the Niger River in 1841.* London: Richard Bentley, 1845.

Allen, William Francis, Charles Pickard Ware, and Lucy McKim Garrison, eds. *Slave Songs of the United States.* New York: A. Simpson, 1867.

Andrews, Garnett. *Reminiscences of an Old Georgia Lawyer.* Atlanta, Georgia: Franklin Steam Printing House, 1870.

Atkins, John. *A Voyage to Guinea, Brasil, and the West Indies. . . .* London: Printed for Ward and Chandler, 1737.

"Baptist: The Negroes in and Around Beaufort, S.C." *Independent* 14 (August 1862).

Barrett, Harris. "Negro Folk Songs." *Southern Workman* 41/4 (April 1912).

Barrow, David. "A Georgia Corn Shucking." *Century Magazine* 24/6 (October 1882).

Bassett, A.L. Ingle. "Going to House Keeping in North Carolina." *Lippincott's Magazine* 28 (August 1881).

————. "Religion in the South: A Negro Revival in Virginia." *Frank Leslie's Illustrated Weekly Newspaper* 36/932 (August 1873).

Benjamin, S. G. W. "The Sea Islands." *Harper's New Monthly Magazine* 57/343 (November 1878).

Bennett, John. "A Revival Sermon at Little St. John's." *Atlantic Monthly* 98 (August 1906).

Bibb, Henry. *Narrative of the Life and Adventures of Henry Bibb, an American Slave. Written by Himself.* New York: The Author, 1849.

Blacknall, O. W. "The New Departure in Negro Life." *Atlantic Monthly* 52 (November 1883).

Bosman, William. *A New and Accurate Description of the Coast of Guinea, Divided into the Gold, the Slave and the Ivory Coast.* London: n.p., 1721.

Bowdich, Thomas Edward. *Mission from Cape Coast Castle to Ashantee.* London: John Murray, 1817.

Boyle, Virginia Frazer. "Old Marse and Aunt Nancy." *Harper's Weekly* 53/2739 (June 1909).

Bremer, Frederika. *Homes of the New World: Impressions of America.* 2 vols. New York: Harper and Brothers, 1853.

Brown, Howard, and Joan Lascelle. *Musical Iconography. . . .* Cambridge, Massachusetts: Harvard University Press, 1972.

Brown, William Wells. *The Anti-Slavery Harp.* Boston: Bela Marsh, 1849.

Burns, Sarah. "Images of Slavery: George Fuller's Depictions of the Antebellum South." *American Art Journal* 15 (Summer 1983).

Cable, George W. "Creole Slave Songs." *Century Magazine* 31/6 (April 1886).

———. "The Dance in Place Congo." *Century Magazine* 31/4 (February 1886).

"Cake Walk, The." *Frank Leslie's Illustrated Weekly Newspaper* 31/796 (December 1870).

Cameron, Rebecca. "Christmas at Buchoi, a North Carolina Rice Plantation." *Ladies Home Journal* (December 1891).

Castellanos, Henry C. *New Orleans as It Was.* New Orleans: L. Graham & Sons, 1895.

Clapperton, Hugh. *Journal of a Second Expedition into the Interior of Africa from the Bight of Benin to Soccatoo.* London: John Murray, 1829.

———, and Dixon Denham. *Narrative of Travels & Discoveries in Northern and Central Africa in the Years 1822, 1823, & 1824 by Major Denham, Captain Clapperton, and the Late Doctor Oudney. . . .* London: John Murray, 1826.

Clarke, W. L. "A Call to Preach." *American Missionary Magazine* 13/2 (February 1869).

Cobb, Joseph Beckham. *Mississippi Sketches; Or, Sketches of Southern and Western Life. . . .* 2d ed. Philadelphia: A. Hart, Late Carey and Hart, 1851.

Coffin, Charles Carleton. *Four Years of Fighting: A Volume of Personal Observation with the Army and Navy, from the First Battle of Bull Run to the Fall of Richmond.* Boston: Ticknor & Fields, 1866.

"Colored Revivals in Virginia." *Frank Leslie's Illustrated Weekly Newspaper* 61/1564 (September 1885).

Conneau, Theophilus. *A Slaver's Log Book, or, Twenty Years' Residence in Africa.* 1854. Edited by Mable M. Smythe. Englewood Cliffs, New Jersey: Prentice Hall, 1976.

Cooley, Stoughton. "The Mississippi Roustabout." *New England Magazine* n.s. 11/3 (November 1894).

"Corn Shuckin' Down South." *New York Sun* (November 1894).

Croome, William H. *City Cries; or, A Peep at Scenes in Town by an Observer.* New York: D. Appleton & Company, 1850.

Crowe, Eyre. *With Thackeray in America.* New York: Charles Scribner's Sons, 1893.

Deming, Clarence. *By-Ways of Nature and Life.* New York: G. P. Putnam's Sons, 1884.

Denham, Dixon, Hugh Clapperton, and Walter Oudney. *Narrative of Travels and Discoveries in Northern and Central Africa in the years 1822, 1823 and 1824. . . .* London: John Murray, 1826.

Donaldson, Mary Katherine. "Paintings and Illustrations of Nineteenth-Century Black Folk Culture in the United States" (Unpublished Paper). Cambridge, Massachusetts: 1986.

Douglass, Frederick. *My Bondage and My Freedom.* New York: Miller, Orton & Mulligan, 1855.

———. *Narrative of the Life of Frederick Douglass, An American Slave. . . .* Boston: Anti-Slavery Office, 1845.

Du Bois, W. E. B. *The Souls of Black Folk.* Chicago: A. C. McClurg & Company, 1903.

Dunbar, Paul Laurence. *In Old Plantation Days.* New York: Dodd, Mead & Company, 1903.

Eiseman, Alvord L. *Charles Demuth.* New York: Watson-Guptill Publications, 1982.

Emery, Lynne Fauley. *Black Dance in the United States from 1619 to 1970.* Palo Alto, California: National Books Press, 1972.

Equiano, Olaudah. *The Interesting Narrative of the Life of Olaudah Equiano, or, Gustavus Vassa, the African. Written by Himself.* New York: Printed and Sold by W. Durell, 1791.

Foner, Philip S. *History of Black Americans.* Westport, Connecticut: Greenwood Press, 1975–83.

Frank Leslie's Illustrated Famous Leaders and Battle Scenes of the Civil War. . . . Edited by Louis Shepheard Moat. New York: Published by Mrs. Frank Leslie, 1896.

Furman, Gabriel. *Antiquities of Long Island.* New York: J. W. Bouton Company, 1875.

Gage, Frances D. "Religious Exercises of the Negroes of the Sea Islands." *Independent* 15 (January 1863).

Genovese, Eugene. *Roll, Jordan, Roll. The World the Slaves Made.* New York: Pantheon Books, 1972.

Gleason, Abbott. "Pavel Svin'in, 1787–1839." *Abroad in America: Visitors to the New Nation, 1776–1914.* Edited by Marc Pachter and Frances Wein. Washington, D.C.: Smithsonian Institution, 1976.

Hawkins, Joseph. *A History of a Voyage to the Coast of Africa, and Travels into the Interior of that Country. . . .* Troy, New York: Printed for the Author by Luther Pratt, 1797.

Hills, Patricia. *Eastman Johnson.* New York: Clarkson N. Potter in association with the Whitney Museum of American Art, 1972.

———. *The Painter's America: Rural and Urban Life, 1810–1910.* New York: Praeger Publishers in association with the Whitney Museum of American Art, 1974.

Hobson, Anne. *In Old Alabama. Being the Chronicle of Miss Mouse, the Little Black Merchant.* New York: Doubleday, Page and Company, 1903.

Hundley, Daniel Robinson. *Social Relations in Our Southern States.* New York: Henry B. Price, 1860.

Hungerford, James. *The Old Plantation, and What I Gathered There in an Autumn Month.* New York: Harper and Brothers, 1859.

Imago musicae. Edited by Tilman Seebass. Published by the International Yearbook of Musical Iconography. Basel, Switzerland: Barenreiter Verlag, 1984–88.

Jacobs, Harriet Brent (Linda Brent). *Incidents in the Life of a Slave Girl. Written by Herself.* Edited by Lydia Maria Child. Boston: Published for the Author, 1861.

Jobson, Richard, *The Golden Trade, or, a Discovery of the River Gambra and the Golden Trade of the Aethiopians.* London: Nicholas Okes, 1623.

Johns, Elizabeth. *American Genre Painting: The Politics of Everyday Life.* New Haven, Connecticut: Yale University Press, 1991.

Johnson, Clifton. *Highways and Byways of the South.* New York: Macmillan Company, 1904.

Jones, Charles Colcock. *Religious Instruction of the Negroes in the United States.* Savannah, Georgia: Thomas Purse, 1842.

"Juba at Vauxhall Gardens, London." *Illustrated London News* (August 1848).

Kaplan, Sidney. *The Portrayal of the Negro in American Painting.* Brunswick, Maine: Bowdoin College Museum of Art, 1964.

Kennedy, John Pendleton. *Swallow Barn; Or, A Sojourn in the Old Dominion.* 1832. Rev. ed. New York: George P. Putnam, 1851.

King, Edward. *The Great South: A Record of Journeys in Louisiana, Texas, the Indian Territory, Missouri. . . .* Hartford, Connecticut: American Publishing Company, 1875.

Kirke, Edmund (pseud. for James Roberts Gilmore). *Among the Pines, or, South in Secession-Time.* New York: J. R. Gilmore, 1862. Also published as *Life in Dixie's Land, or, South in Secession-Time.* London: Ward & Lock, 1863.

Laing, Alexander Gordon. *Travels in the Timannee, Kooranko, and Soolima Countries in Western Africa.* London: John Murray, 1825.

Latrobe, Benjamin Henry. *The Journal of Latrobe . . . Notes and Sketches. . . . from 1796 to 1820.* With an Introduction by J.H.B. Latrobe. New York: D. Appleton, 1905.

Leiding, Harriette Kershaw. *Street Cries of an Old Southern City.* Charleston, South Carolina: Press of the Dragget Printing Company, 1910.

Le Page du Pratz, Antoine Simon. *The History of Louisiana, or of the Western Parts of Virginia and Carolina. . . .* London: Printed for T. Becket, 1774.

Leppert, Richard. *Music and Image . . .* New York: Cambridge University Press, 1988.

"Life and Travel in the Southern States." *Great Republic Monthly* 1 (1859). Reprint in *Travels in the Old South Selected from Periodicals of the Time.* Edited by Eugene L. Schwaab and Jacqueline Bull. Vol. 2. Lexington: University of Kentucky, 1973.

Long, John Dixon. *Pictures of Slavery in Church and State. . . .* Philadelphia: Published by the Author, 1857.

Malsby, M. A. "A Prayer Meeting at a Corn Shucking." *Southern Christian Advocate* 23/3 (January 1860).

Marryat, Frederick. *A Diary in America with Remarks on Its Institutions.* London: Printed for Longman, Orme, Brown, Green and Longman, 1839.

McElroy, Guy C. *Facing History: The Black Image in American Art, 1710–1940.* San Francisco,

California: Bedford Arts, publishers, in association with the Corcoran Gallery of Art, 1990.

Mead, Whitman. *Travels in North America.* New York: Printed by C. S. Van Winkle, 1820.

Milburn, William Henry. *Ten Years of Preacher-Life; Or, Chapters from an Autobiography.* New York: Derby & Jackson, 1859.

Moderwell, Hiram Kelly. "The Epic of the Black Man." *New Republic* (September 1917).

Moore, Francis. *Travels into the Inland Parts of Africa . . . Containing a Description of the Several Nations for the Space of 600 Miles up the River Gambia.* London: n.p., 1737.

Mordecai, Samuel. *Richmond in By-Gone Days; Being Reminiscences of an Old Citizen.* Richmond, Virginia: G. M. West, 1856.

Moreau de Saint-Mery, Mederic Louis Elie. *Dance.* Philadelphia: Published by the Author, 1796.

Munsell, Joel. *Collections on the History of Albany from Its Discovery to the Present Time. . . .* 4 vols. Albany, New York: J. Munsell, 1865–71.

Murphy, Jeanette Robinson. "The True Negro Music and Its Decline." *Independent* 55/2851 (July 1903).

"Musical Gleanings in Africa." *Harmonicon* 3/28 (April 1825).

"Musical Gleanings in Africa." *Harmonicon* 4/41 (May 1826).

"Negro Fables." *Riverside Magazine for Young People* 4 (November 1868; March 1869; April 1870).

Northup, Soloman. *Twelve Years a Slave. . . . Kidnapped in Washington City in 1841, and Rescued in 1853. . . .* Auburn, New York: Derby and Miller, 1853.

"Noted Pennsylvania Prison." *Frank Leslie's Illustrated Weekly Newspaper* 56/1433 (March 1883).

Old Dominion in the Seventeenth Century, The. A Documentary History of Virginia, 1606–1689. Edited by Warren Billings. Chapel Hill: University of North Carolina Press, 1975.

"Old Landmark, An." *Harper's Weekly* 18 (June 1874).

"On the Observation Platform of a Vestibe Train, Entering Charleston, S.C.—Music by the 'Bottle Band.' " *Frank Leslie's Illustrated Weekly Newspaper* 68/1745 (February 1889).

Paine, Lewis W. *Six Years in a Georgia Prison.* New York: Printed for the Author, 1851.

Panofsky, Erwin. "Iconography and Iconology. . . ." *Meaning in the Visual Arts* (1939). Garden City, New York: Doubleday & Company, 1955.

Patten, J. Alexander. "Scenes from Lynchburg." *Travels in the Old South* 2. Edited by Eugene L. Schwaab and Jacqueline Bull. Lexington: University Press of Kentucky, 1973.

Pendleton, Louis. "Salmagundi: 'Black' Corinth Church." *Southern Bivouac* n. s. 2/6 (November 1886).

Pierson, Hamilton W. *In the Brush; Or, Old-Time Social, Political, and Religious Life in the Southwest.* New York: D. Appleton & Company, 1881.

Platt, Orville. "Negro Governors." *Papers of the New Haven Colony Historical Society* 6 (1900).

Poesch, Jessie. *The Art of the Old South.* New York: Alfred A. Knopf, 1983.

"Professors of Chin-Music." *Frank Leslie's Illustrated Weekly Newspaper* 32/827 (August 1871).

Raboteau, Albert J. *Slave Religion: The "Invisible Institution" in the Antebellum South.* New York: Oxford University Press, 1978.

Ravenel, Henry William. "Recollections of Southern Plantation Life." *Yale Review* 25 (June 1936).

"Religious Trust among the Contrabands." *National Anti-Slavery Standard* 22/1105 (August 1861).

Rexford, Eben E. "Negro Music." *Musical Visitor* 21/4 (April 1897).

Roy, Joseph E. "Studies in the South: Negro Prayer Meeting." *American Missionary Magazine* n.s., 36/10 (October 1882).

"Scene from Richmond [Virginia], A." *Christian Watchman & Reflector* (*Watchman-Examiner*) 49 (July 1868).

"Scenes at the South." *Frank Leslie's Illustrated Weekly Newspaper* 56/1432 (March 1883).

Scharf, John Thomas, and Thompson Westcott. *History of Philadelphia, 1609–1884.* Philadelphia: L. H. Everts & Company, 1884.

Shanley, C. D. "The Street Cries of New York." *Atlantic Monthly* 25/148 (February 1870).

Smith, William. *A Voyage to Guinea: Describing the Customs, Manners, Soil, Climate . . . and Whatever Else Memorable among the Inhabitants.* London: Printed for John Nource, 1744.

Smyth, John F. *A Tour in the United States of America.* London: Printed for G. Robinson, 1784.

"Song of the Oystermen." *Frank Leslie's Illustrated Weekly Newspaper* 51/1308 (October 1880).

Southern, Eileen. *The Music of Black Americans: A History.* 1971. Rev. ed. New York: W. W. Norton and Company, 1983.

———, ed. *Readings in Black American Music.* New York: W. W. Norton & Company, 1971.

———, and Josephine Wright. *African-American Traditions in Song, Sermon, Tale, and Dance, 1600s–1920: An Annotated Bibliography of Literature, Collections, and Artworks.* Westport, Connecticut: Greenwood Publishing Group, 1990.

Stuart, Isaac William [pseud. Scaeva.]. *Hartford in the Olden Time: Its First Thirty Years.* . . . Hartford, Connecticut: F. A. Brown, 1853.

Svin'in, Pavel Petrovich. *Picturesque United States of America, 1811, 1812, 1813 . . . Containing Copious Excerpts from His Account of Travels in America.* . . . Edited and translated by Avrahm Yarmolinsky. New York: W. E. Rudge, 1930.

Thompson, Maurice. "Plantation Music." *Critic* 4/99 (January 1884).

"Virginia Tobacco Mart, A." *Harper's Weekly* 23/1166 (May 1879).

"Virginia Watch Meeting." *Frank Leslie's Illustrated Weekly Newspaper* 49/1267 (January 1880).

"Waifs: The Old African Church in Richmond, Virginia." *Musical World* (New York) 61 (April 1873).

"Wandering Minstrels on Harlem Lane." *Frank Leslie's Weekly Illustrated Newspaper* 34/862 (April 1872).

Warren, Edward. *A Doctor's Experiences in Three Continents.* Baltimore, Maryland: Cushings & Bailey, 1885.

Watson, John Fanning. *Annals of Philadelphia and Pennsylvania in the Olden Time.* . . . 2 vols. Philadelphia: Elijah Thomas, 1857.

———, *Methodist Error* (1819). Reprint in Eileen Southern, ed. *Readings in Black American Music* 62–64 (New York: W. W. Norton and Company, 1971).

Williams, Isaac D. *Sunshine and Shadow of Slave Life.* East Saginaw, Michigan: Evening News Printing and Building House, 1885.

Index of Artwork by Title

Index of Artists

Subject Index